Ancient Classics for English Readers

EDITED BY THE

REV. W. LUCAS COLLINS, M.A.

(SUPPLEMENTARY SERIES.)

DEMOSTHENES

The Volumes published of this Series contain

HOMER: THE ILIAD, BY THE EDITOR.
HOMER: THE ODYSSEY, BY THE SAME.
HERODOTUS, BY GEORGE C. SWAYNE, M.A.
CÆSAR, BY ANTHONY TROLLOPE.
VIRGIL, BY THE EDITOR.
HORACE, BY THEODORE MARTIN.
ÆSCHYLUS, BY REGINALD S. COPLESTON, M.A.
XENOPHON, BY SIR ALEX. GRANT, BART., LL.D.
CICERO, BY THE EDITOR.
SOPHOCLES, BY CLIFTON W. COLLINS, M.A.
PLINY, BY A. CHURCH, M.A., AND W. J. BRODRIBB, M.A.
EURIPIDES, BY WILLIAM BODHAM DONNE.
JUVENAL, BY EDWARD WALFORD, M.A.
ARISTOPHANES, BY THE EDITOR.
HESIOD AND THEOGNIS, BY JAMES DAVIES, M.A.
PLAUTUS AND TERENCE, BY THE EDITOR.
TACITUS, BY WILLIAM BODHAM DONNE.
LUCIAN, BY THE EDITOR.
PLATO, BY CLIFTON W. COLLINS.
THE GREEK ANTHOLOGY, BY LORD NEAVES.

SUPPLEMENTARY SERIES.

The Volumes now published contain

1. LIVY, BY THE REV. W. LUCAS COLLINS, M.A.
2. OVID, BY THE REV. A. CHURCH, M.A.
3. CATULLUS, TIBULLUS, & PROPERTIUS, BY THE REV. JAMES DAVIES, M.A.
4. DEMOSTHENES, BY THE REV. W. J. BRODRIBB, M.A.

Other Volumes are in preparation.

DEMOSTHENES

BY THE

Rev. W. J. BRODRIBB, M.A.

LATE FELLOW OF ST JOHN'S COLLEGE,
CAMBRIDGE

PHILADELPHIA:

J. B. LIPPINCOTT & CO.

1877.

NOTE.

FOR the extracts from the speeches of Demosthenes
given in this volume I am to a considerable extent
indebted to the scholarly version of the late Mr C. R.
Kennedy. For the famous speech on the Crown, I
have made occasional use of a translation recently
published by an eminent English lawyer, the Right
Hon. Sir Robert Collier. The same speech was, some
years ago, translated by Mr William Brandt, a scholar
of Oriel College, Oxford, whose premature death cut
short a life of great promise. His rendering of the
Greek orator is spirited and vigorous, and I wish to
express my obligations to it.

W. J. B.

9337

CONTENTS.

			PAGE
INTRODUCTION,	. . . .	.	1
CHAP.	I.	GREECE IN THE FOURTH CENTURY B.C.,	.	4
"	II.	MACEDON AND PHILIP, . . .	.	13
"	III.	EARLY LIFE OF DEMOSTHENES, . .	.	22
"	IV.	DEMOSTHENES ENTERS POLITICAL LIFE,	.	32
"	V.	EARLY SPEECHES OF DEMOSTHENES ON FOREIGN POLICY, ...	44
"	VI.	FIRST SPEECH OF DEMOSTHENES AGAINST PHILIP — SPEECH FOR THE FREEDOM OF THE PEOPLE OF RHODES, . . .	57
"	VII.	PHILIP AND OLYNTHUS—SPEECHES OF DEMOSTHENES ON BEHALF OF THE OLYNTHIANS,	72
"	VIII.	DEMOSTHENES AND MEIDIAS, . . .	84
"	IX.	PHILIP MASTER OF THERMOPYLÆ AND OF PHOCIS—PEACE BETWEEN HIM AND ATHENS —COUNSEL OF DEMOSTHENES, . . .	92
"	X.	DEMOSTHENES CONTINUES HIS SPEECHES AGAINST PHILIP, ...	102
"	XI.	CHÆRONEIA—FALL OF GREECE, . . .	122
"	XII.	CONTEST BETWEEN DEMOSTHENES AND ÆSCHINES, ...	135
"	XIII.	LAST DAYS OF DEMOSTHENES, . . .	147
"	XIV.	DEMOSTHENES AT THE BAR, . . .	153
		CONCLUSION, ...	172

MAP: GREECE AND ITS ADJACENT ISLANDS.

DEMOSTHENES.

INTRODUCTION.

THE familiar names of Demosthenes and Cicero will always be linked together. They are specially representative names. The eloquence of the ancient world seems to be summed up in them. There is a further reason why we should think of them together. Both attached themselves to a falling cause; both had to go into exile; both had the satisfaction of being welcomed back from exile; both, finally, when all was lost, were willing to die rather than survive their country's disgrace. There is, indeed, a striking resemblance between the lives and fortunes of the two men, and none of Plutarch's parallels is more appropriate than that in which he has compared them.

The best and noblest eloquence must be the product of earnest political conviction. Cicero clung to the traditions of the old republic, and regarded the concentration of power in one man as equivalent to his country's degradation and fall. The Greek statesman could not imagine a worse calamity than that Greece should cease to exist as an aggregate of free, self-governing communities, and become a dependency on a foreign kingdom or empire. We cannot but sympathise with such a sentiment. It was a noble one, though at the time it may have been becoming more and more incapable of realisation, as indeed was the sincere belief of some perfectly honest men who were politically opposed to Demosthenes. The highest aspects of Greek life, and its best influences on the civilisation of the world, were intimately connected with Greece as existing according to his conception of what she ought to be. His eloquence is at its highest when he dwells on her fixed resolution in past days to resist to the death anything like foreign dictation or interference. Greece, in his view, was nothing if she once brought herself to endure it.

On the whole, perhaps the Greek was rather a greater figure than the Roman orator. He was at least more single-minded and courageous. His political career was more dignified and consistent, and there were fewer weak moments in his life. Cicero, it is true, was a singularly amiable and a most accomplished man ; but he was unquestionably vain and self-complacent. Demosthenes gives us the idea that Athens and Greece were always foremost in his thoughts. As an orator and statesman he may claim to rank above Cicero. As an orator, he was the master of a more fervid and impressive eloquence ; as a statesman, he had more simplicity of purpose and greater moral courage.

The period of Demosthenes is the fourth century B.C.
A brief sketch of it seems almost due to our readers.
The speeches of Demosthenes cannot be understood
without some acquaintance with Greek politics. Macedon, too, and its rise to importance under king Philip,
deserves at least a short notice. The history of the
time is somewhat intricate, and could not be thoroughly
elucidated in a very moderate compass. An endeavour
has been made in the two following chapters to present the reader with a view of its general character.

CHAPTER I.

ATHENS in the fifth century B.C. was at the head of the Greek world. Her empire, like our own, was a "government of dependencies." In its nature it was somewhat precarious. Although it was not specially oppressive, it was in many quarters an object of extreme jealousy. When Athens attempted the conquest of Sicily, it was felt that this was but a step towards ulterior and more dangerous designs. It was a most hazardous attempt, under existing circumstances. On the sea, indeed, Athens was all-powerful; but she had formidable enemies on land very near her—Thebes to the north, Sparta to the south. After her great reverse in Sicily, she was hardly a match for Sparta at the head of the Peloponnese. She still struggled on, and even won some victories, till the long contest, known as the Peloponnesian War, came to an end in 405 B.C. with the decisive battle of Ægos-potami. There, in the waters of the Hellespont, almost her entire fleet was captured by the Spartan admiral, Lysander.

Sparta now succeeded to the headship of Greece. She retained it down to the year 371 B.C. During this period she contrived to make herself thoroughly hated. Her system was to rule by means of oligarchical factions in the different states. These factions she supported by military garrisons. There was a garrison for a time in the Cadmea, or the citadel of Thebes. It was forced into the city, and subsequently maintained there with a flagrant disregard of justice and equity. The Spartan king Agesilaus coolly asserted that if it was for Sparta's interest it was right. Altogether, the Spartan rule was much more galling than the Athenian had been. Sparta, indeed, always seems to have been a more selfish state than Athens. It is true that Athens in her greatness had been spoken of as " a despot city;" but there was at the same time a feeling that she worthily represented Greece. This could hardly be said of Sparta. She was now cultivating friendly relations with Persia, and had procured the conclusion of a peace with that power, the terms of which were by no means honourable to Greece. This was the peace of Antalcidas in 387 B.C.—one of the landmarks, so to say, in Greek history. It had ever been a Greek tradition that the freedom and independence of the Greeks in Asia ought to be upheld. By the peace of Antalcidas they were put under the dominion of Persia. Athens would hardly have yielded such a point, and in the days of her maritime supremacy she could and would have made it impossible. Sparta was responsible for this disgraceful concession. She made matters worse by seeking to convert her headship of Greece into a downright despotism. In doing this she wrought infinite mischief, and may be almost said to have pre-

pared the way for the subsequent calamities of Greece
and its subjection to Macedon. She endeavoured persistently to break up the Greek world into a number
of petty dependencies, which she might hold under
her absolute control. Her systematic policy was to
reduce Greece to a collection of separate towns and
even villages, each of which should be completely in
her own power. The idea which lay at the root of
Greek strength and greatness was, that Greece should
be made up of federations, with the leading cities at
the head of them. In the face of a common foe these
federations, it was hoped and believed, would be at-
tracted to each other, and would feel that they had a
common cause. This was Panhellenism. Sparta, by
her methods of rule, weakened this idea, and thereby
undermined the foundations of the Greek world. The
feebleness and disunion of Greece in the fourth century
B.C., which were so favourable to Macedon, were, in
part at least, due to Sparta's influence. In one instance she inflicted the most direct and positive mischief
upon Greece. At the head of the Gulf of Torone, in
the peninsula of Chalcidice, was the prosperous city of
Olynthus, round which had grown up a confederacy
of Greek towns that might have been an effectual
barrier against Macedon, or any other northern power.
This confederacy Sparta, true to her policy, broke up
in 379 B.C., and thus gave a heavy blow to Greek interests on the coasts of Macedon and Thrace. But for
this, the Ægean and the Propontis might never have
known the presence of Macedonian cruisers, and Philip's
kingdom might have remained a poor and barbarous

territory. Olynthus, indeed, to a certain extent recovered herself, and became again a flourishing and
independent city; but the mischief which had been
already done was past remedy.

With the great battle of Leuctra in 371 B.C. Sparta's
ascendancy ceased. Thebes was now raised by the
illustrious Epameinondas into the first place in Greece.
North of the Peloponnese she could do as she pleased.
She had Thessaly quite under her control, and Macedon
was little better than a dependency. Her next step,
after Leuctra, was to strengthen herself in the Peloponnese, and to complete the humiliation of Sparta. This
was done by the founding of the two cities Megalopolis
and Messene, under the direction of Epameinondas.
Sparta, as we have seen, aimed at breaking up and dissolving federations; Thebes, on the contrary, formed
the Arcadian townships, forty in number, into a confederacy, of which Megalopolis, the Great City, was
made the centre. Messene was then founded on Mount
Ithome, and became the rallying-place of a population
which had long been unwillingly subject to Sparta.
What had hitherto been Spartan territory was actually
annexed to it. Sparta's limits were thus greatly nar-
rowed. On the north and or th west she was con-
fronted by independent communities, and her position
in the Peloponnese was wellnigh destroyed. Though
Thebes soon fell back from the pre-eminence to which
the genius of Epameinondas had lifted her, Sparta was
never able to regain her ancient *prestige*.

Athens, from some cause or other, had much more
elasticity and power of recovery than Sparta. There

was a life and sprightliness about her citizens which
made them quickly forget calamities and rise to new
hopes and aspirations. So it was with them after
Leuctra. Athens at once was fired with the ambition
of winning back her old empire; and she actually succeeded in again becoming the head of a powerful confederacy. The disgust which Sparta had provoked
throughout the Greek world was no doubt a great help
to Athens. Once more her fleet sailed supreme over
the Ægean. As a matter of course, the chief islands
joined her alliance. A synod of deputies from her allies
and dependents obeyed her summons, and contributions were voted for the common cause. She had able
men—such as Timotheus, Iphicrates, and Chabrias—
to command her forces. At the time of Philip's accession to the throne of Macedon in 359 B.C., Athens was
the first state in Greece. She was not specially well
fitted for war on land, and was in this respect inferior
to Thebes, which could send out an army in the highest
efficiency. But by sea she was, beyond comparison,
the first power. Rhodes, Chios, Cos, and the important
cities of Perinthus and Byzantium, were her allies.
Samos, off the coast of Lydia, and Thasos, Lemnos,
Imbros in the north of the Ægean, had been recently
conquered by her; she was in possession of the Thracian Chersonese, of Pydna and Methone on the coast
of Macedon, and of Potidæa and other towns in the
peninsula of Chalcidice. The waters of the Ægean
were thus an Athenian lake. But she could not hold
together this confederation. She had no proper control
over her generals. They were not in fact the servants

of the state, but men of the "Condottieri" type. As a rule, they commanded mercenaries, for whom they could not provide pay without systematically plundering the allies. These generals really maintained their troops by means of "forced benevolences." It could hardly be expected that all this would be patiently endured. In 358 B.C. the Social War, as it was termed, broke out—Rhodes and Byzantium, it would seem, leading the revolt. It lasted two years. The efforts of Athens appear to have been rather fitful and wanting in vigour. When a rumour came that Persia was about to support the revolted allies with a fleet of 300 ships, Athens gave up the struggle and acknowledged their independence. The confederation, of which for a brief space she had been the head, was thus at an end.

This was a great blow to Athens. She was still powerful by sea, but she was very much impoverished, a large part of her revenue having been lost to her through the secession of several of her richest allies. Was it not now best for her to rest from her ambition, and to think no more of "a spirited foreign policy"? So argued one of her citizens, the famous orator Isocrates. He complains that his countrymen "were so infatuated that while they themselves wanted the means of subsistence they were undertaking to maintain mercenaries, and were maltreating their allies and levying tribute from them, in order that they might provide pay for the common enemies of mankind." By these he means the generals, of whom also Demosthenes, his political opponent, says, in one of his speeches, that "they go ranging about and behaving everywhere as the common enemies of all who wish to live in freedom according to their own laws." Athens, he contends, might recover from the losses and disasters of the Social War, if she would only eschew for the future a meddling and aggressive policy, be prepared for self-defence, and devote herself to commerce and to the arts of peace. In this way she would, with the great natural advantages she possessed, very soon again become rich and prosperous. This was the advice of Isocrates. It might well seem sensible and timely. And, as a matter of fact, it suited the temper of many of the citizens. There was a disposition to shrink from personal efforts, and, if war became a necessity, to leave it more and more to mercenaries. In such a mood there were dangers, as the event proved, to the cause both of Athens and of Greece.

A peace party was the natural result. It was in power at Athens for some years after the conclusion of the Social war, the critical period during which Philip of Macedon was step by step advancing to the position he ultimately attained. It had the advocacy of the speeches and pamphlets of Isocrates, who had the command, not undeservedly, of the public ear. It was thus supported by the ablest journalism of the day. Again, it had an eminently respectable man as one of its leaders. This was Phocion, whose integrity was proverbial. Forty-five times was he chosen general, and he gained several victories for Athens. He was alone sufficient to give strength to a political party. Another of its leaders was Eubulus, a man of very inferior type. His great aim was to put the people in a good humour. There was a singular arrangement at Athens by which the State defrayed the cost of the public amusements and dramatic exhibitions for the benefit of the poor citizens. A regular fund was provided for this purpose, and after a time the surplus of the annual public revenue was added to it. It had formerly been the law that this surplus should always during war be paid into the military chest for the defence of the State. Eubulus actually induced the people to pass a law making it a capital offence to propose that this fund should be so applied on any future occasion. Consequently, the only method of meeting the costs of war was the exaction of a property tax from the rich. War under these circumstances could not but involve very serious and sorely-felt sacrifices. We may form some idea of the pressure of the burden by supposing the case of an income tax of 4s. or 5s. in the pound among ourselves. No ministry, it is clear, could venture to declare war except under the most palpable necessity, if such a tax were inevitable. Eubulus accordingly conciliated the rich by doing his utmost to save them from the dreaded burden. He was, as we should say, prime minister of Athens for sixteen years. His position must have been a very strong one, acceptable, as we have just seen, to rich and poor alike. There can hardly be a doubt that his policy impaired the Athenian character, and made the work of Demosthenes peculiarly difficult.

Athens thus entered on a great contest under unfavourable conditions. She was still, from her extensive trade, the richest city in Greece, and she had the means of sending out formidable fleets. But her citizens liked ease and comfort, and preferred their cheerful city life to foreign service. Her dominions, too, were rather vulnerable, not being guarded by any regular troops. If they were attacked, they had to be defended by mercenaries, commanded by the sort of general who. has been described. Then, too, her commerce, with which her prosperity was closely bound up, might be harassed by an enterprising enemy, and her supplies of corn from the Black Sea endangered. Thus, in fighting Macedon she was perhaps at some disadvantage, though we may be inclined to think that a little more energy and vigour would have carried her successfully through the struggle. The truth is, she was not for a long time alive to the real danger, and was consequently remiss in seizing opportunities. There was a party which urged alliance with Thebes. But Thebes was more hateful to an average Athenian than Sparta had ever been. Such a party seemed untrue to the old traditions of Athens. Hence it was always comparatively weak. Had the danger from Macedon been distinctly foreseen, the alliance would perhaps have been effected. Athens and Thebes united might, it can hardly be doubted, have confined Philip to his own hereditary kingdom and have saved Greece.

CHAPTER II.

MACEDON AND PHILIP.

THE name of Macedon, though it is heard of from time to time in Greek history, can hardly be said to have become really famous till the fourth century B.C. and the reign of Philip. It could never have occurred to the mind of a Greek that this outlying northern kingdom might possibly one day be formidable to Greece and its freedom. There were no signs pointing in this direction; and it may be fairly assumed that no political sagacity could have foreseen such a result. The Macedonians were always looked upon by the Greeks as barbarians, although their royal family—Temenids, as they were called, from their legendary ancestor, Temenus—came from Argos, and the people themselves perhaps had some distant affinity to the Hellenic race. For a long period they were nothing better than a collection of rude tribes, with scarcely any cohesion or organisation, and before the disciplined army of a Greek state they would have been utterly powerless. They were surrounded, too, by fierce and unquiet neighbours—Illyrians to the west, Pæonians to the north, Thracians to the east,—all savage, warlike peoples, whom they could only just hold in check. The country, indeed, with its rivers and rich valleys and strips of seaboard, had natural advantages which a vigorous prince with organising capacity might develop; and this was partially done by Archelaus, who reigned from 413 B.C. to 399. He was a man of great energy, and he may be said to have put Macedon in the way to become a flourishing and powerful kingdom. According to Thucydides,* he had roads constructed, fortresses erected, and established a standing army on a greater scale than any of his predecessors had kept up. Probably the last years of the Peloponnesian war, which were so disastrous to Athens, were favourable to Macedon, and enabled it to acquire an influence on the northern coasts of the Ægean, which previously Athens had possessed. Still, no doubt Archelaus deserves the credit of having steadily applied himself to the work of strengthening and consolidating his kingdom. At the same time, he did his best to civilise his people, and to bring them into connection with the Greek world. He cultivated the friendship of Athens, and sought to introduce its literature and art. He established a grand periodical festival on the Greek type, with all the humanising adjuncts of music and poetry. The great poet Euripides visited his court at his special invitation, and was treated with such favour and respect that he remained there till his death. The philosopher Socrates was invited, but it appears that he declined the honour. The famous painter, Zeuxis of Heracleia, was one of the king's guests, and he was employed to adorn with pic-

* Thucydides, ii. 100.

tures the royal palace at Pella, the new capital of Macedonia. In fact, Archelaus was an enlightened despot; and though he could not eradicate barbarism and make Macedonians into Greeks, he at least gave the higher class a varnish of Greek civilisation and culture.

It was not unusual for the kings of Macedon to perish by the hands of conspirators and assassins, and this was the fate of Archelaus. The dynasty was now changed; and after a few years of disturbance, Amyntas, the father of Philip, became king in 394 B.C. His reign was not a prosperous one. Macedonia went back, and its very existence as an independent kingdom was in jeopardy. According to one account, Amyntas was obliged to surrender Philip as a hostage to the Illyrians, who were then particularly troublesome. He left his kingdom at his death, in 370 B.C., in an almost desperate plight. The succession to the throne was disputed, and the enemies on the border were as formidable as ever. Macedon, indeed, seemed on the eve of being wholly extinguished. The eldest son and successor of Amyntas, Alexander, was murdered; and shortly afterwards the Theban Pelopidas was invited into the country by the friends of the royal family, with the view probably of securing the throne for the two younger brothers, Perdiccas and Philip. Pelopidas, it seems, forced on Macedonia the adoption of this arrangement, and took Philip with him to Thebes, as a hostage for its being faithfully carried out. Philip passed three years at Thebes, while his brother Perdiccas was king. He then, in 368 B.C., was intrusted

with the government of a portion of Macedonia under
Perdiccas, and employed his time in equipping and
organising some troops. His brother's reign had a disastrous termination. He was defeated with heavy loss
by the Illyrians, and died soon afterwards. And so
Philip, now twenty-three years of age, became king of
Macedon in 359 B.C., there being only an infant son
of Perdiccas whose claim to the throne it was not difficult, under the circumstances, to set aside with the
national approval.

No prince could have begun his reign with gloomier
prospects than the future conqueror of Greece. He
was encompassed by enemies. There were other claim-
ants of the throne—one of these being Argæus, who
was supported by Athens. He thus had to fear attack
from barbarian neighbours by land, and from Athenian
fleets by sea. The hostile attitude of the Athenians
was determined by their very prudent desire to recover
the important position of Amphipolis at the mouth of
the Strymon. To Athens the possession of this place
was of the utmost value, as it was the key to a region
rich in gold and silver mines, as well as in forest-timber.
To this the people had an eye, in supporting the pre-
tensions of Argæus to the throne of Macedon against
Philip. The king, however, met them promptly, and
won a victory over a little force which they had sent
to Methone on the Macedonian coast of the Gulf of
Thermæ. He took some Athenian citizens prisoners ;
but as he was anxious to conciliate Athens, he treated
them with marked respect, and allowed them at once
to return. He then made peace with Athens, and

waived all claim to Amphipolis, in which his pre-
decessor had placed a Macedonian garrison. The city
was now left to itself; and the Athenians, had they
been wise, would have spared no effort to secure it.
As it was, they let slip a golden opportunity of regain-
ing a position which might have been in their hands a
barrier against the growing power of Macedon, and
would have certainly enabled them to maintain their
maritime supremacy on the Ægean.

Philip meanwhile, having freed himself for the
present from the fear of Athens, was at liberty to fence
off his kingdom from the attacks of its land enemies.
He had already organised something of a military force,
and with this he prepared to strike a decisive blow at
the Illyrian, Pæonian, and Thracian tribes, which were
perpetually crossing the Macedonian frontier in plundering expeditions. It seems that these tribes, which
were scattered over what are now the provinces of
Bosnia, Servia, and Albania, were at this time being
pushed southwards by a great movement of the Gauls.
The Illyrians were Macedon's most dangerous neighbours, and they had inflicted many a disastrous defeat
on Philip's predecessors. Now they were at the height
of their power, and were united for purposes of war
under a chief named Bardylis, an able leader and a
brave warrior. Philip, after thoroughly vanquishing
the Pæonians, which he seems to have done easily,
turned his arms against the more formidable Illyrians,
and attacked them in western Macedonia, which they
had invaded. He won a hard-fought battle, chiefly
through the efficiency of his cavalry. The Illyrian

army was utterly discomfited, and their chief was glad to make peace, and cede whatever portions of Macedonia he had conquered and occupied. The result of this victory was, that the Macedonian frontier was pushed to the lake Lychnitis (now Okridha), and was made far more secure than it had hitherto been, by the occupation of mountain-passes through which the Illyrian invaders used to pour into Macedonia.

The famous phalanx, which we connect specially with the names of Macedon and Philip and Alexander, is said to have taken part in this battle. Philip has been credited with this military invention; but, in truth, he can be said only to have introduced it. He may have considerably modified it, but it had always been an important element in a Greek army. It was the great Epameinondas of Thebes who seems to have first organised it in its most powerful and effective form. He, in fact, it was who brought the science of war to the highest perfection hitherto known in Greece. Philip, during his residence as a young man in Thebes, may well have had opportunities of personal intercourse with this illustrious general, and have derived from him many profitable hints and suggestions. At all events, he had daily under his eyes the magnificent soldiers who had fought and conquered at Leuctra. His first military ideas were thus drawn from the best of all schools, and we may well suppose that a deep impression was at the same time made on his young imagination. He would soon see that the barbarous enemies of Macedon would never be able to stand against really well-trained troops. He had also at Thebes the literary and philosophical

teaching which often lays the foundation of able statesmanship. Possibly he may have made the acquaintance
of Plato, and there is certainly ground for believing
that the philosopher conceived a high opinion of his
ability. Nor is it unlikely that he may also at this
time have had his admiration directed by some circum-
stance to Aristotle, whom he afterwards made the
tutor of the young Alexander. It is certain that he
became imbued with some amount of Greek culture,
and that he acquired the power of speaking and writing
the language almost as well as a professed orator or
rhetorician. He liked to look on himself, and to be
regarded by others, as thoroughly a Greek; and this it
was, no doubt, which inclined him to be always con-
siderate towards Athens, as the foremost state of Greece.
Perhaps he was not too young, before he left Thebes,
to imbibe some political notions. In such a city he
would at least have a good opportunity of getting an
insight into the character of Greek politics, and he
might have early learnt some of those weak points in
Greece which his adroitness subsequently enabled him
to turn to such profitable account.

Philip, after his victories over the Illyrians and
Pæonians, which for a time at least made Macedonia
secure on the land side, still reigned over a poor and
half-barbarous kingdom. He had much to do before
he could hope to become a considerable power in the
Greek world. As yet, he did not possess a single town
on the coast. He had, as we have seen, given up
Amphipolis to please the Athenians. He must have
been surprised to find that they did not make haste to

recover that important place. But they committed the blunder, and allowed the people of Amphipolis to remain their own masters. Soon afterwards, in 358 B.C., Philip thought he might as well possess himself of it; and when the inhabitants refused to surrender, he laid siege to the city. Envoys were sent to Athens, asking for help; but it is possible that at this crisis the war with the allies had just begun, and that the Athenians may have thus found themselves fully occupied. Philip, too, promised them in a very civil letter that he would put them in possession of it as soon as he had taken it. The Athenians did nothing, though it could not have been very difficult for them to have saved the place and secured it for themselves. This was indeed short-sighted, as they now again had an opportunity of securing a commanding position, and of nipping Philip's power in the bud. It was one of those errors which can never be retrieved. Athens lost *prestige*, as well as a most useful dependency. When Philip took the city, Olynthus, which was not far distant, and was at the head of a group of Greek townships in the peninsula of Chalcidice, was seriously alarmed, and proposed an alliance to Athens. The offer was rejected, as the Athenians, it seems, still wished to look on Philip as their friend, and were persuaded to trust his promises. The cunning prince contrived not only to buy off the hostility of Olynthus, but actually to win its friendship and to become its ally by the cession of a disputed strip of territory near Thessalonica. The next thing he did was to venture on an openly hostile act against Athens by conquering and wresting from her a most important possession, the city of Potidæa, on the gulf of Thermæ. This, too, he gave up to the Olynthians. Pydna, also, on the shore of the same gulf, opposite to Potidæa, likewise an Athenian possession, fell into his hands through internal treachery; and Athens, it appears, made no effort to save the place. Thus, in a single year, 358 B.C., Philip gained three most valuable positions on the coast, and a severe shock was given to Athenian influence in the north of the Ægean. He had hitherto been poor; now he had the means of raising an ample revenue. Master of Amphipolis, he had free access to the gold region in the neighbourhood east of the Strymon. Here he founded the city which we know by the familiar name of Philippi. He had now a well-organised army, and he was able to maintain it. In little more than two years he had immensely increased the strength and resources of his kingdom. But it was not till six years afterwards that Macedon was felt to be a distinct menace to the Greek world.

CHAPTER III.

EARLY LIFE OF DEMOSTHENES.

WE cannot be quite certain about the year in which Demosthenes was born. The accounts are conflicting, and we are thrown back on somewhat doubtful inferences. The year, it seems, must have been either 385-384 B.C. or 382-381 B.C. His early life thus coincided with an eventful period, and witnessed more than one remarkable political change in the Greek world. In the years immediately after his birth the supremacy of Sparta was unquestioned. Greece lay at her feet. Her power had made itself felt far beyond the Peloponnese, even on the northern shores of the Ægean. She had overthrown the city which might have become an effectual bulwark against the terrible king of Macedon. Olynthus became her vassal in the year 379 B.C. All was changed eight years afterwards. The decisive battle of Leuctra, in 371 B.C., struck down Sparta and gave the ascendancy to Thebes. For a few years Greece resounded with the fame of her two illustrious citzens, Epameinondas and Pelopidas. But when she lost Epameinondas, nine years after Leuctra, in the brilliant victory of Mantineia, she lost with him the supreme control of Greek politics, retaining merely the foremost rank among the northern states. Meanwhile she had given, as we have seen, shelter and education to the future destroyer of Greek freedom.

Amid these changes and revolutions, Demosthenes grew up to manhood. His own state, Athens, had achieved nothing specially worthy of record during this period. Still, she was altogether the most famous city of Greece, and was commercially prosperous. The father of Demosthenes, who bore the same name, was a rich and eminently respectable citizen. He was a merchant and a manufacturer, and belonged to the wealthy middle class. His property was distributed in various investments. He had two manufactories, and each, it seems, had a good business. One was a sword and knife manufactory, and employed thirty-two slaves. The other was a cabinet manufactory, and in this twenty slaves were employed. He had also money out at interest, a deposit account at one of the principal banks, and sums lent, according to a very prevalent Athenian practice, on ship-cargoes. He had, too, a house of some value, and good furniture and plate ; and his wife was an heiress, and had her jewels on a tolerably handsome scale. But the lady, whose name was Cleobule, was not of pure Athenian blood, and her birth and antecedents were not quite what could be desired. Her father, Gylon, was a man of distinctly blemished reputation. He had been, in fact, accused of treason—the charge against him being that he had betrayed to the enemy the seaport town of Nymphæum in the Crimea. He did not appear to answer the accusation, and was, according to one account, sentenced to death in his absence. But he contrived to do well for himself. He went to Panticapæum, now Kertch, in the Crimea, then the capital of the kings of Bosporus, and there, through the king's favour, obtained a grant of land and married a rich wife. She was sneeringly spoken of at Athens as a barbarian and a Scythian—and so Æschines describes her; but it is quite possible that she may have been the daughter of one of those many Greeks who had settled in this remote district to carry on the business of exporting corn to Athens. It was then, as now, a specially corn-growing region. Gylon, it seems, made the most of the king's favour, and traded with great success. He was unquestionably a sharp, shrewd man; and he sent his two daughters well dowered to Athens, and there they both made fairly good matches. Both got Athenian citizens for their husbands—the one marrying Demochares, and the other the elder Demosthenes. We may not unreasonably conjecture that the mother of Demosthenes inherited some natural ability from her sagacious and enterprising father.

It was the misfortune of Demosthenes to be left an orphan when only seven years of age, and to fall into the hands of unscrupulous guardians. His father died worth fourteen talents,—about £3500 of our money. This, according to modern notions, is a very moderate property; but at Athens it was sufficiently large to place its possessor in the wealthiest class, and to render him liable to the highest rate of direct taxation. There were much larger fortunes, no doubt, as that of Nicias,

which is said to have amounted to 100 talents, or about
£24,000. Alcibiades was even richer; and Callias, who
lived at the time of the Persian war, and secured a
good share of the plunder, was what we should call a
millionaire, being reported to have been worth 200
talents. Athens, as we have seen, was, of all the Greek
cities, by far the richest, and it always contained a
number of well-to-do citizens. The ordinary rate of
interest was extremely high. Money lent even on good
security fetched from 12 to 20 per cent; and some investments, those especially on ship-cargoes—hazardous,
no doubt—were yet more lucrative. As much as 30
per cent was now and then paid on this class of investments. Demosthenes asserts, in his pleadings against
his guardians, that a third part of his estate produced
an income of fifty minas. This would make the
entire income about £600 a-year. Now, it appears that
a citizen could live just decently at Athens on something like seven or eight minas a-year, or about £32;
and in perfect comfort and respectability on fifty
minas, or about £200 a-year, provided he kept clear of
the various costly public services which were demanded
from the rich. Demosthenes, therefore, it is clear,
having but one sister, ought to have had a very ample
fortune, though he could not have been described as
extremely wealthy. His father, being in business,
probably got 25 or even 30 per cent for a large part
of his capital, and we should suppose that he was at
Athens in much the same position as a man with from
£2000 to £3000 a-year would be with us. Had his
will been faithfully carried out, and a third of the

income been set apart for maintenance and education, and two-thirds profitably invested, the son must have been decidedly rich when at the age of sixteen, ten years after his father's death, he attained his majority.

As it was, he found himself comparatively poor. He had to receive something less than two talents, and his income could not have exceeded from £60 to £70 a-year. His father, we may surmise, had misgivings about the administration of the property, as he practically endeavoured to bribe the three guardians, two of whom were his nephews, into a faithful discharge of their trust by giving them full control over almost one-third of the property. His sister's son, Aphobus, was to marry the widow, with a fair fortune, and to have the house and furniture during the minority of Demosthenes. His brother's son, Demophon, was to have two talents,˙ and to marry the daughter in due time. In all respects he seems to have carefully provided for his two children, and to have left them in the charge of relatives on whose fidelity he might reasonably reckon. The result can be ascribed only to negligence and dishonesty. The property must have been partly muddled away, partly actually embezzled. Admitting that some of the investments were precarious, and that the business of the two manufactories was simply mismanaged, we can hardly doubt that the trustees were unprincipled as well as utterly careless. It is true, indeed, that Demosthenes was taunted by his rival Æschines with having squandered his patrimony in ridiculous follies; and it was alleged by one of the guardians, in defending the action, that large advances had been made. **The** boy had, it would seem, rather luxurious tastes, and in the last two years of his minority he may have indulged them freely. But this very inadequately explains the smallness of the sums handed over to him. It is an all but absolute certainty that he was swindled out of his property. The matter ended in his bringing an action against Aphobus, and recovering a verdict for ten talents. It is not certain whether he actually received this amount. Aphobus was rich and influential, and contrived to make further difficulties. We have five speeches connected with this action—three against Aphobus, and two against a brother-in-law of Aphobus, Onetor. It is from these speeches that we chiefly get our information about the property of Demosthenes. We have not the means of knowing the precise results of the suit, or what benefit, if any, Demosthenes derived from it. Much of the estate had somehow or other disappeared, and he had to enter on life as rather a poor instead of a rich man.

It is probable that his misfortunes had a good effect on his character. They may have been the source of his intense resolution and perseverance. From early years he had a weak constitution, and shrank from the vigorous physical training which was considered an essential element in a Greek education. He had an active mind, and a strong craving for intellectual culture. As became his position and expectations, he went to good schools—though his guardians, if we may believe his statement, were shabby enough to leave his school-fees unpaid. He had a passion for speeches and recitations; and it was said that he once induced his schoolmaster to go with him to hear one of the first speakers of the day, Callistratus, who was delivering a great political harangue on the cession of the border-town Oropus to the Thebans. The occasion may have been a turning-point in his life. But he had an unlucky infirmity; he, who was to be the greatest orator of all time, stammered in his boyhood and youth. It would seem as if his physical defects were too much for his mental vigour and his ambitious aspirations.

Plutarch in his 'Life of Demosthenes' gives us several interesting details about his study and preparation for the career of an orator, and it is satisfactory to find that so high an authority as Mr Grote thinks that they rest on good evidence. It appears that the youth put himself under the instruction of Isæus, one of the first advocates of the time, who was frequently retained in cases connected with wills and disputes about property. In his speeches against his guardians he is said to have availed himself of the counsel and guidance of this eminent lawyer. But the most fashionable rhetoric-professor of the day was Isocrates, and Demosthenes was among the number of his most attentive and ad-miring hearers; though perhaps we must not believe a story according to which he asked the great man to teach him a fifth part of his art for two minas, as he could not afford the regular fee of ten minas, about £40, to learn the whole. One would like to believe that he heard and admired some of the discourses of Plato, who was then in the height of his philosophical glory; and there is a tradition, mentioned by Cicero and Tacitus, to this effect. The literary styles of the

two men are no doubt very diverse; yet, as Dr Thirlwall suggests, it is not wholly improbable that the
lofty morality which Demosthenes ventured to introduce into speeches addressed to Athenian assemblies
and law courts may have been inspired by the philosopher. That he was a devoted student of the great
History of Thucydides, that he copied it out eight times,
and almost knew it by heart, we may well believe.
One of the ancient critics, Dionysius of Halycarnassus,
has elaborately pointed out resemblances in the orator
to the historian. Strangely enough Cicero, in his
Orator,* asks the question, "What Greek orator ever
borrowed anything from Thucydides?" We really fail
to see the point of this question, unless he meant to
limit the term orator to a mere pleader, and even then
we think he is wrong. But for the purpose of political
oratory there cannot be a doubt that both the style and
matter of Thucydides might be studied with infinite
profit by a man of real capacity.

Nothing but the utmost energy and perseverance
would have enabled Demosthenes to make himself an
orator. He had, as already said, to surmount the
actual physical difficulties of a feeble constitution and
of some defect in his organs of speech. His ultimate
success was a decisive proof of a singularly exceptional
force of character. It is for this, indeed, as exhibited
throughout his whole career, that he specially deserves
admiration. We are told that he practised speaking
with pebbles in his mouth; that he strengthened his
lungs and his voice by reciting as he ran up hill; that

* Chapter ix.

he declaimed on the seashore amid the noise of waves and storms. He would even pass two or three months continuously in a subterranean cell, shaving one side of his head, that he might not be able to show himself in public, to the interruption of his rhetorical exercises. But all this patient and laborious practice did not procure immediate success. No public assembly could be more critical and fastidious than that of Athens. Demosthenes failed repeatedly. One of the old citizens found him on one of these occasions wandering about disconsolately in the Piræus, and tried to cheer him up by saying, " You have a way of speaking which reminds me of Pericles, but you lose yourself through mere timidity and cowardice." Another time he was returning to his home in deep dejection, when Satyrus, a great and popular actor, with whom he was well acquainted, entered into conversation with him. Demosthenes complained that though he was the most painstaking of all the orators, and had almost sacrificed his health to his intense application, yet he could find no favour with the people, and that drunken seamen and other illiterate persons were listened to in preference to himself. " True," replied the actor, " but I will provide you a remedy if you will repeat to me some speech in Euripides or Sophocles." Demosthenes did so, and then Satyrus recited the same speech in such a manner that it seemed to the orator quite a different passage. With the aid of such hints, joined to his own indefatigable industry, he at last achieved a distinct success in the law courts, and his services as an advocate were in great request.

After all, he had not much of which, according to

our notions, a man could reasonably complain. Success came to him very early in life. He was, as we should say, in large practice at the bar when he was considerably under thirty—an age at which a young English barrister hardly hopes for a brief. Doubtless, at Athens there were opportunities for displaying oratorical ability which do not exist in England. One thoroughly successful speech before the popular assembly might well make the fortune of a man as an advocate. To make such a speech required, we may be sure, marked ability and considerable training; but once made, it must at least have opened a career in the law courts. Athenian law, too, was probably less intricate and difficult than English. It had not such a variety of branches, as seem to be indispensable in so complex a community as our own. The study of it must thus have been a much less arduous task than that which lies before the English lawyer. But it was an admirable preparation for political life. Law and politics were intermingled at Athens very much more than among ourselves; and a lawyer was almost necessarily something of a politician. There, questions which we regard as purely political, and which would be discussed with us only in Parliament, might come before a law court. An accusation, for instance, might be preferred against a man for proposing a law or a decree quite at variance with the spirit of the constitution. Such cases were frequent. It was in a prosecution of this nature that Demosthenes, who for some few years had had a good practice as a barrister in civil and criminal causes, made what we may fairly call his first appearance as a political adviser.

CHAPTER IV.

DEMOSTHENES ENTERS POLITICAL LIFE.

In all democracies much will be expected from the rich. This was the rule in the Greek states, and especially at Athens. There the constitution demanded a certain amount of public spirit, and prescribed various modes in which it was to display itself. Athenians loved a bright joyous life, and the wealthier of them were under legal obligations to minister to the popular tastes and contribute to the public amusements. There was a good side to all this. It made the rich feel that they must not use their riches merely for their own selfish enjoyment, but that it ought to be the glory of an Athenian citizen of fortune to put happiness and refinement within the reach of every member of the community. Pericles, in the famous funeral oration, the substance of which Thucydides has given us, had boasted how it was the peculiar genius of Athens to combine mirthfulness and gaiety with a strong sense of political responsibility.

Poetry and music were an essential part of an Athenian's life. They were intimately connected with all the religious festivals. With us the pleasures of the opera are necessarily confined to a select few. At

Athens the poorest citizen was enabled to gratify his taste for such pleasures. The law imposed on a man with a certain amount of property the liability of having to provide a chorus of singers or musicians on some great public occasion. He had to bear all the expenses himself. Having made up his number, he had to obtain a teacher or choir-master, and to pay him for his instruction. He had also, it seems, to board and lodge the chorus during the time of its training, and he had, further, to furnish them with suitable dresses. All this, of course, he could do by deputy; but if he was anxious, as he usually would be, to do it with credit to himself, he would find that he must give the matter his personal attention. There was a prize for the best performance; and this, if not intrinsically valuable, was sure to be coveted. The choragus, as he was called, had a stall assigned him in the theatre, and it was part of his duty to be present during the ceremony with his crown and robe of office. There seems to have been every variety of chorus—tragic and comic choruses, pyrrhic choruses, and choruses of flute-players. The expense of providing them might range from £100 to £1200—a large sum in comparison with Athenian wealth. Still this amount was, it appears, often exceeded in an eager competition for the prize. The successful choragus was certain to be a popular citizen.

This, then, was one of the regular charges on the wealthier class. There were others. Athleticism and gymnastic games were a prominent feature in Greek life. At Athens one of the amusements in which they specially delighted was running with the torch, the runners carrying wax lights in their hands, which it was their object not to extinguish. The race in the time of Socrates began to be run on horseback, and the training and preparation for it became one of the public services, which the rich had to undertake. The gymnasiarch, or director of these games, had to defray all the expenses connected with the spectacle ; he had to see to and to pay for the training of the competitors, which was on a very elaborate scale, and might involve a comparatively heavy outlay. Another still more burdensome obligation was the conduct of religious embassies to various places. This was regarded as a duty of the highest and most sacred kind ; and whenever the State sent out a special commission to any of the ancient seats of Greek worship, such as Delos or Delphi, to consult the oracle of the god or to offer a solemn sacrifice, it was represented by citizens of wealth and distinction. Anything like parsimony on such an occasion would have been thought peculiarly discreditable, and it was the tendency of an Athenian to go to the opposite extreme. The head of the sacred mission entered the city whither he was bound with a crown of gold and in a splendidly equipped chariot. Alcibiades astonished the Greek world at the Olympic festival with his magnificent horses and his princely expenditure. Even in an ordinary way, however, the performance of this duty must have been a costly service. A minor expense was that of giving a public dinner to the particular tribe of which a man was a member. This too was a burden imposed on the rich. Last of all came the obligation to maintain the fleet in efficiency,—Athens' defence and glory. This—the trierarchy, as it was called—was a service of which we are continually hearing in the speeches of Demosthenes, and to place it on a satisfactory footing was an object he had specially at heart.

All these services, it must be understood, were legally compulsory—not merely enforced on the rich by public opinion, as in our time. At Athens, no citizen who was registered as the possessor of a certain amount of property could evade them. A man in England may be obliged to serve the office of sheriff once in a way, but to try to create public spirit by law would be repugnant to our notions. In a Greek state there was a much more distinct theory as to what each citizen owed to the commonwealth; and Athens, the very type of Greek democracy, felt it most natural to make these demands on her richer classes. At the same time, she had thought fit to exempt certain persons from the operation of this principle. There were a few whose meritorious services might be fairly considered to have earned them such an exemption—the trierarchy alone excepted The privilege in some cases was extended to their descendants. Two names were cherished at Athens with peculiarly grateful remembrance, those of Harmodius and Aristogeiton, the illustrious tyrannicides, who were believed to have given freedom and equality to their city. To their offspring for ever was granted immunity from the public burdens we have just described. In like manner, a statesman or a general who had deserved well of his country might be rewarded with the same privilege for himself and

his children.　With us such men occasionally obtain
pensions, which, in a few instances, are continued to
their descendants.　With the Athenians, they enjoyed
what was perhaps almost an equivalent—exemption
from costly and burdensome services.

It is easy to see that many abuses might creep into
this system; and that even without any very glaring
abuses, there might be much envy and dissatisfaction.
Privileges of any kind are sure to give offence, and in
a democratical community they cannot fail to furnish a
handle to demagogues and politicians.　We are therefore not surprised to find that at Athens in 356 B.C. a
law was proposed and carried repealing all exemptions
and immunities.　The author of the law was a certain
Leptines, who was no doubt put forward as the spokes-
man of a considerable party.　He contrived to get a
measure of a very sweeping kind passed, so that not
only were all existing grants of immunity abolished,
but it was declared illegal to make such grants in the
future, and even to ask for them was forbidden under
a heavy penalty.　We do not know whether there was
any special impulse or provocation under which the
people of Athens allowed themselves to be persuaded
into passing this law.　It roused, of course, a strong
opposition, the leader of which was a son of the famous
Chabrias, who had fallen in his country's cause, fighting
on board his ship at the siege of Chios.　The son had
inherited from his father one of these honourable grants
of immunity.　He was, it seems, himself utterly unworthy of it; but he represented a principle, and had,
we may be sure, a numerous following.　Demosthenes

became his advocate, and in the year subsequent to the passing of the law, he assailed it in a speech which has always been much admired.

This was his first political effort. He was quite a young man at the time—thirty years of age at most, probably less. The speech he delivered does not exhibit the fire and force of some of his subsequent orations; it is calm and argumentative, and deserves the epithet of "subtle" which Cicero * applies to it. It is in fact a specimen throughout of close and consecutive reasoning. Leptines' proposal was no doubt popular, and it was supported by many plausible arguments. The circumstances of the State were such as made any exemptions and immunities from public burdens of very questionable expediency. Athens had been seriously impoverished by her recent disastrous war with her allies, and many of her richer citizens must, for a time at least, have been sorely straitened in their resources. To exempt such wealthy men from burdens which there was not too much wealth left to bear, might well seem a distinct loss to the State. It increased the difficulty of providing for those public festivals which were so dear to the people. It could also no doubt be plausibly argued that exemptions had been granted too freely, and now and then to thoroughly unworthy persons. Many a man not particularly rich would think himself aggrieved, when he saw some one far richer than himself altogether exempt. The favoured few were sure to be envied, and might almost be said to be defrauding the State of what they owed it. The

* **Orator,** c. xxxi.

object, in fact, of the law of Leptines was, it might be contended, to insure for Athens the due performance of services which she had a right to claim from every citizen of ample means. The burden, he argued, ought to fall on all such ; no exemptions ought to be granted, as it was likely they would be granted unwisely, and the examples of other states, such as Sparta and Thebes, showed that these grants were unnecessary. Besides, merit at Athens was rewarded in other ways ; and in sweeping away such rewards as these, they would be really abolishing what was not needed by the possessors, and was at the same time injurious to the State. Thus the new law seemed on the surface a good one, and must have enlisted popular sympathy. It promised to get rid of invidious privileges, to distribute public burdens equitably, and to provide for the celebration of the festivals and games with becoming splendour.

The occasion was thus clearly one to task all the powers of an opposition speaker. If we want a modern analogy, we may suppose a motion brought forward in the House of Commons in a time of national distress, when every tax would be acutely felt, to abolish all pensions ever granted to deserving men and to their children. It is conceivable that such a proposition might find supporters at a trying crisis, and become a powerful party-cry. Demosthenes may well have had an uphill battle to fight. But he took the right ground, and rested his case on the highest moral principles and the most enlightened view of political expediency. The faith and honour of the State, he maintained, must be superior to all other considerations. We may say that the text of his speech was—" A good name is better than riches."

First, he argued that it was unjust to deprive the people of the power to grant special privileges because they had sometimes granted them improperly.

" You might as well take from them all their constitutional rights because they do not always exercise them wisely. Even if a few undeserving persons received these privileges, this was better than that none should be conferred, and that a powerful encouragement to patriotism should be withdrawn. To revoke gifts which the State had bestowed would be a scandalous breach of the national faith. It would cast a slur on democratic government, and create an impression that such governments were as little to be trusted as those of oligarchs and despots. It would be base ingratitude to many distinguished foreigners—for example, to the king of Bosporus, from whose country much corn was exported to Athens, free of duty—and such men for the future would not care to befriend the State in a time of need. It was nothing to the purpose to speak of Sparta and Thebes, as proofs that these grants of exemption were not required. The whole genius and character of those states were so radically different, that no conclusion could be reasonably drawn from them as to what suited Athenians. It was of supreme importance that Athens, as the noblest representative of Greece, should value above all things a character for justice, generosity, and public spirit. To attempt to bind her for all future time by a law which might be a hurtful and dangerous check on patriotic impulses must be inexpedient. No one could foresee what course politics might take, and it was possible that citizens like Harmodius and Aristogeiton might again be needed. All human legislation must take account of such possibilities and contingencies, improbable as they might seem at the time. The law of Leptines was, in fact, an offence to Nemesis, which ever waits on arrogance and presumption."

These were some of the chief arguments with which Demosthenes combated the reasonings of his opponent. In one passage he reminds his audience how careful Athens had been in the past of her good name.

"You have to consider not merely whether you love money, but whether you love also a good name, which you are more anxious after than money; and not you only, but your ancestors, as I can prove. For when they had got wealth in abundance, they expended it all in pursuit of honour. For glory's sake they never shrank from any danger, but persevered to the last, spending even their private fortunes. Instead of a good name, this law fastens an opprobrium on the commonwealth, unworthy both of your ancestors and yourselves. It begets three of the greatest reproaches—the reputation of being envious, faithless, and ungrateful. That it is altogether foreign to your character to establish a law like this, I will endeavour to prove in a few words by recounting one of the former acts of the State. The Thirty Tyrants are said to have borrowed money from the Lacedæmonians to attack the party in the

Piræus. When unanimity was restored, and these troubles were composed, the Lacedæmonians sent ambassadors and demanded payment of their money. Upon this there arose a debate, and some contended that the borrowers, the city party, should pay; others advised that it should be the first proof of harmony to join in discharging the debt. The people, we know, determined themselves to contribute, and share in the expense, to avoid breaking any article of their convention. Then, were it not shameful if, at that time, you chose to contribute money for the benefit of persons who had injured you, rather than break your word, yet now, when it is in your power, without cost, to do justice to your benefactors by repealing this law, you should prefer to break your word?"

He argues that the envious, grudging spirit displayed in the law is, of all things, most alien to Athenian feeling.

"Every possible reproach should be avoided, but most of all, that of being envious. Why? Because envy is altogether the mark of a bad disposition, and to have this feeling is wholly unpardonable. Besides, abhorring, as our commonwealth does, everything disgraceful, there is no reproach from which she is further removed than from the imputation of being envious. Observe how strong are the proofs. In the first place, you are the only people who have state funerals for the dead, and funeral orations in which you glorify the actions of brave men. Such a custom is that of a people which admires virtue, and does not envy others who are honoured for it. In the next place, you have ever bestowed the highest rewards upon those who win the garlands in gymnastic contests; nor have you, because but few are born to partake of such rewards, envied the parties receiving them, nor abridged your honours on that account. Add to these striking evidences that no one appears ever to have surpassed our State in liberality—such munificence has she displayed in requiting services. All these are manifestations of justice, virtue, magnanimity. Do not destroy the character for which our State has all along been renowned; do not, in order that Leptines may wreak his personal malice upon some whom he dislikes, deprive the State and yourselves of the honourable name which you have enjoyed throughout all time. Regard this as a contest purely for the dignity of Athens, whether it is to be maintained the same as before, or to be impaired and degraded."

The following passage is near the conclusion of the speech. He is arguing against the impolicy of binding the State for the future by such a law :—

"To one thing more I beg your attention. This law cannot be good which makes the same provision for the future as the past. 'No one shall be exempt,' it says, 'not even the descendants of Harmodius and Aristogeiton.' Good. 'Nor shall it be lawful to grant exemptions hereafter.' Not if similar men arise? Blame former doings as you may, know you also the future? Oh, but we are far from expecting anything of the kind. I trust we are; but being human, our language and our law should be such as not to shock religious sentiment; and while we look for good fortune, and implore heaven to grant it, we will regard all fortune as subject to human casualties. The future, I take it, is uncertain to all men, and small occasions are productive of great events. Therefore we will be moderate in prosperity, and show that we have an eye to the future."

It may be said that there is much of a modern tone and character about this speech. Its arguments are those of a constitutional lawyer and of a far-sighted politician. It is quiet and temperate, and at the same time singularly convincing. It was successful in its immediate object, and it must have established the reputation of Demosthenes as a political debater of the first rank. From this time he must have felt but little timidity or hesitation in addressing that critical audience—the Athenian popular assembly.

CHAPTER V.

PERSIA in the fourth century B.C. was a more co
able power than we might have supposed fr
comparative ease with which it was overthro
Alexander. The Great King, as he was always
was in the possession of immense resources. Fina
he was much stronger than the Greek world, tho
military inferiority had been ·more than once
proved. He was still looked on by the Greeks g
with a sort of wondering awe. He ruled in some
a vast empire, and held it together by means o
and vassal princes, notwithstanding occasiona
revolts. He had had indeed, in past days, to
ledge the independence of the Asiatic Greeks
was always distinctly felt as a force in Greek
with which from time to time he was brought into
contact. On the whole, he was regarded as an enemy;
but the unfortunate want of anything like hearty union
among the states of Greece tended to weaken this feeling, and to make combined action against him all but
impossible. There was always, however, a vague fear
that he might some day, if violently provoked, crush

the Greek world beneath the weight of a huge barbarian invasion.

In the year 356 B.C., the second year of Athens' war with her revolted allies, this fear rose, at Athens at least, to a positive panic. Greek generals, as we have seen, occasionally found it convenient to take service under some Persian satrap, for the sake of the liberal pay on which they could confidently reckon. In the year above mentioned, Chares was in command of a fleet which Athens had sent out to put down her rebellious subjects in the islands of the Ægean. He was a man thoroughly of the adventurer type; and when he found that he could not pay his troops, which were for the most part foreign mercenaries, he carried off his armament on his own responsibility to the aid of Artabanus, the satrap of the country south of the Propontis, who was then in revolt against the Great King. Artabanus was, at the time, in sore need of help; but Chares gained for him a brilliant victory over the king's forces, and he received for himself and his soldiers a liberal reward. The proceeding was, of course, utterly irregular, and gave great offence at Athens; but the success reconciled them to it. The King of Persia was naturally very indignant, and sent an embassy to Athens to complain of this unprovoked aggression. Soon it was rumoured that he was preparing a fleet of 300 galleys to aid their revolted allies and to attack their city. There was intense excitement. Peace was immediately concluded with the allies, but there was a strong feeling in favour of declaring war against Persia. Now, it was said, was the time for an appeal to Panhellenic sentiment, and to endeavour to unite Greece against her old enemy. We can well imagine that such language was likely to meet with a response in many quarters, and that it might well seem patriotic, and even prudent.

In this case, again, Demosthenes thought it his duty to protest. He did so in a speech delivered in 354 B.C. He must have been, in all probability, on the unpopular side. He had, too, against him the opinion of the famous and clever rhetorician, Isocrates, who had urged in one of his pamphlets the expediency of a Panhellenic combination against Persia. The party of Eubulus, backed up by a number of orators and demagogues, supported this policy. To Demosthenes it seemed an idle dream—the preposterous imagination of a knot of political adventurers. The speech in which he opposed it is calm and statesmanlike. "In no one of his speeches," says Mr Grote, "is the spirit of practical wisdom more predominant than in this his earliest known discourse to the public Assembly." He tells his excited countrymen some very plain home-truths. "The Greeks," he frankly says, "are too jealous of each other to be capable of uniting in an aggressive war. They might indeed do so in a war of self-defence. Should Athens declare war, the King of Persia would be able to purchase aid from the Greeks themselves. Such a step would consequently lay bare the worst weaknesses of the Greek world. Their right policy was to put Athens in a posture of defence, that she might not be attacked unprepared. They must re-organise their fleet. They must not shrink from personal military service and lean upon foreign mercenaries.

They must not rest contentedly on the glorious deeds of their ancestors, but uphold the dignity of their State by themselves imitating their deeds, whatever temporary sacrifices it might cost them. And they should seek to rally round Athens a host of confederates, united to her by the bonds of common interest and mutual confidence." Some of these topics are such as, under critical circumstances, it must have required much moral courage to urge.

A few passages from the speech will give the reader an idea of Demosthenes' views about Persia, about the difficulty of united action against that power, and the immediate duties of the Athenians themselves :—

" I hold the King," he says, " to be the common enemy of all the Greeks. Still I would not for this reason advise you without the rest to undertake a war against him. The Greeks themselves, I observe, are not friends to one another. On the contrary, some have more confidence in the King than in certain of their own people. Such being the case, I deem it expedient for you to see that the cause of war be equitable and just, that all necessary preparations be made, and that this should be the groundwork of your resolution. Were there any plain proof that the King of Persia was about to attack the Greeks, I think they would join alliance, and be extremely grateful to those who sided with them and defended them against him. But if we rush into a quarrel before his intentions are declared, I am afraid that we shall be driven into a war with both—with the King and with the people whom we are anxious to protect. He will suspend his designs, if he really has resolved to attack the Greeks, will give money to some, and promise friendship; while they, in the wish to carry on their own wars with better success and intent on similar objects, will disregard the common safety of the Greek world. I beseech you not to betray our country into such embarrassment and folly. You, I perceive, cannot adopt the same policy in regard to the king as the other Greeks can. Many of them, I conceive, may very well pursue their selfish interests, and be utterly indifferent to the national welfare. But for you it would be dishonourable, even though you had suffered wrong, so to punish the wrong-doers as to let any of them fall under the power of the barbarian. Under these circumstances we must be careful not to engage in the war on unequal terms, and not to allow him whom we suppose to be planning mischief against the Greeks to get the credit of appearing their friend."

Although Athens is rich, he warns the people that those riches will not be forthcoming on a mere vague rumour of hostilities from Persia. When the danger is seen to be really imminent, then it will be time for the State to put a pressure on its wealthy citizens.

"You invite the Greeks to join you. But if you will not act as they wish, how can you expect they will obey your call, when some of them have no good-will towards you? Because, forsooth, they will hear from you that Persia has designs on them? Pray, do you imagine that they don't foresee it themselves? I am sure they do; but at present the fear outweighs the enmity which some of them bear towards you and towards each other. Athens contains treasures equal to the rest of the Greek states put together. But the owners of wealth are so minded that if all your orators alarmed them with the intelligence that the King was coming, that he was at hand, that the danger was inevitable—if, besides the orators, a number of persons gave oracular warning—so far from contributing, they would not even discover their wealth or acknowledge its possession. But if they knew that what is so terrible in report was really begun, there is not a man so foolish who would not be ready to give and foremost to contribute. I say that we have money against the time of actual need, but not before. And therefore I advise you not to search for it now. Your right course is to complete your other preparations. Let the rich retain their riches for the present (it cannot be in better hands for the State); and should the crisis come, then take it from them in voluntary contributions."

The speech is thus concluded :—

"My advice is, do not be over-alarmed at the war; neither be led to commence it. As far as I see, no other state of Greece has reason to fear it. All the Greeks know that so long as they regarded Persia as their common enemy, they were at peace one with another, and enjoyed much prosperity. But since they have looked on the King as a friend, and quarrelled about disputes with each other, they have suffered worse calamities than any one could possibly imprecate upon them. Should we fear a man whom both fortune and heaven declare to be an unprofitable friend and a useful enemy? If it were possible with one heart and with united forces to attack him alone, such an injury I could not pronounce to be an injustice. But since this cannot be, I say we must be cautious, and not afford the King a pretence for vindicating the rights of the other Greeks. Do not expose the melancholy condition of Greece by convoking her people when you cannot persuade them, and making war when you cannot carry it on. Only keep quiet, fear nothing, and prepare yourselves. My advice in brief is this: Prepare yourselves against existing enemies; and you ought with the same force to be able to resist the King and all others, if they attempt to injure you. But never begin a wrong in word or deed. Let us look that our actions, and not our speeches on the platform, be worthy of our ancestors. If you pursue this course, you will do service not only to yourselves, but also to those who give the opposite counsel; for you will not be angry with them afterwards for errors now committed."

In this speech Demosthenes may be said to foreshadow the general character of his foreign policy. He did not wish Athens to be aggressive, but simply to hold her own with a firm hand. This, he thought, she might well be persuaded to do. Grand schemes of Panhellenic union against the empire of Persia, such as floated before the imagination of Isocrates, and were, through his influence, fascinating the minds of a certain class of political enthusiasts, he scouted as Quixotic. Above all things, he aimed at being a practical statesman; and of this the speech from which we have just been quoting, delivered by him in the commencement of his public life, is decisive evidence.

In the following year he delivered a speech which is of considerable interest as showing his view of Greek politics at the time. It was important, he thought, for Athens that there should be, as we say, a balance of power in the Greek world, and that neither Sparta nor Thebes should be too strong. I have explained the circumstances under which Megalopolis was founded in 371 B.C., after the great battle of Leuctra, under Theban influence, as the metropolis of Arcadia, and specially as a check on Sparta. The establishment of this city, together with the loss of the Messenian territory, which soon followed, was a terrible blow to that state. Sparta, in fact, for the time, was reduced to a second-rate power. She was hemmed in by enemies on the north and on the west. It was hardly to be expected that she would acquiesce in such humiliation. And so, in the year 353 B.C., her king, Archidamus, began to plan a counter-revolution, which should undo the work of Leuctra by the destruction of Megalopolis and the reconquest of Messenia. It was, however, necessary for him to have some pretext which should commend itself generally to Greek opinion. He was meditating an entire unsettlement of the affairs of the Peloponnese in the interest of Sparta; and this, he knew, would not be allowed if it were to be openly

avowed. Accordingly he put forward the policy of a
general restoration of ancient rights to the different
states. Athens would thus recover the border town of
Oropus, now in the possession of Thebes, the loss of
which had much vexed and distressed her. Thus, it
was hoped, she might be disposed to favour the Spartan proposals, which, as a matter of course, the anti-
Theban party, then very strong, would back up to the
utmost of its power. The result which such a policy
would have on Megalopolis, as a barrier in Sparta's
way, was kept in the background. The new city must
have inevitably dwindled down into an insignificant
township, and the purpose with which it had been
founded would have been frustrated.

Envoys came to Athens both from Sparta and from
Megalopolis. There was a warm and angry debate.
The bitter hatred Athenians had always felt towards
Thebans, coupled with the immediate desire of recovering Oropus, was enough to recommend the Spartan
proposals. It seems strange that the memory of what
Athens had suffered from the hands of Sparta did not
at once decide the question, and open the eyes of the
people to the dangers of Sparta's insidious policy.
Some there were who saw through it and denounced
it. Demosthenes was among the number. He was
with the "Opposition;" and it appears that on this
occasion he failed. He supported the cause of Megalopolis—the cause, in fact, of Thebes—arguing that it
would be a grave political blunder to assist Sparta in
recovering the position which she held in Greece previous to the battle of Leuctra. His speech is subtle

and ingenious, and must have been convincing to those who would not let themselves be carried away by an unreasoning antipathy to everything Theban.

"The Lacedæmonians," he says, "are acting a crafty part. They say they cannot retain the gratitude they feel for you for helping them in a time of urgent need unless you now allow them to commit an injustice. However repugnant it may be to the designs of the Spartans that we should adopt the Arcadian alliance" (that is, the alliance of Megalopolis), "surely their gratitude for having been saved by us in a crisis of extreme peril ought to outweigh their resentment for being checked in their aggression now."

As to the bait held out by Sparta to Athens in the prospect of the recovery of Oropus, he says :—

"My opinion is, first, that our State, even without sacrificing any Arcadian people to the Lacedæmonians, may recover Oropus, both with their aid, if they are minded to act justly, and that of others who hold Theban usurpation to be intolerable. Secondly, supposing that it were evident to us that, unless we permit the Lacedæmonians to reduce the Peloponnese, we cannot obtain possession of Oropus, allow me to say, I deem it more expedient to let Oropus alone than to abandon Messenia and the Peloponnese to the Lacedæmonians. I imagine the question between us and them would soon be about other matters. . . .

"I am sure, to judge from rational observation— and I think most Athenians will agree with me—that if the Lacedæmonians take Megalopolis, Messenia will be in danger; and if they take Messenia, I predict that you and the Thebans will be allies. Then it is much better and more honourable for us to receive the Theban confederacy as our friends and resist Lacedæmonian ambition, than, out of reluctance to save the allies of Thebes, to abandon them now, and have afterwards to save Thebes herself and be in fear also for our own safety. I cannot but regard it as perilous to our State should the Lacedæmonians take Megalopolis and again become strong. For I see they have undertaken the war not to defend themselves, but to recover their ancient power. What were their designs when they possessed that power, you perhaps know better than I, and therefore may have reason to be alarmed."

This was plain speaking, and sound, statesmanlike advice. It could not have been the interest of Athens to let Sparta regain her old supremacy, as she was certainly striving to do. It was her interest, as Demosthenes says towards the conclusion of his speech, not to abandon Megalopolis and the Arcadians, and to make them feel (should they survive the struggle) that they had owed their deliverance not to themselves or to any other people but the Athenians. As affairs turned out, the dangers he apprehended never came to pass. He could not persuade his countrymen to support Megalopolis. They simply stood neutral. The Lacedæmonians waged war for two years in Arcadia, and gained some partial successes, but they could not carry out their designs. Thebes, though she had occupation

for her soldiers in other quarters, contrived to send
an army into the Peloponnese; and after some inde-
cisive engagements, a truce was concluded, which left
matters as they were. Megalopolis and the Arcadian
confederacy escaped the peril with which Sparta had
threatened them. But the result to Athens and to
Greece was unsatisfactory. Subsequently, when they
apprehended a similar danger from Sparta, they did
not think it worth their while to ask help from Athens.
They did not care to be refused a second time, and on
this occasion they applied to Philip. He was not the
man to miss such an opportunity; and thus Macedonian influence was brought to bear on the affairs of
the Peloponnese. This was the unfortunate consequence of the indifference of Athens to the progress
of Spartan ambition. She gave the impression to the
Greek world that she was not in earnest in wishing to
maintain the liberties of the states of the Peloponnese,
although it had been her constant profession to do so.
This was the inference drawn from her refusal to ally
herself with Megalopolis against Sparta. Had she
been guided by the counsels of Demosthenes, she
would have assumed a dignified political attitude, and,
as events turned out, have put a stumbling-block in
the way of her future enemy and destroyer. It is
true, indeed, that at that time there was no distinct
cause of apprehension from Macedon, and there is not
even any allusion to Philip in this speech of Demosthenes. We may therefore conclude that as yet he
himself feared nothing in that quarter. Still, it is not
the less to his credit that he urged Athens to adopt a

policy which would have won for her the respect and
confidence of many of the Greeks, and might have had
the effect of excluding the intrusion of a most dangerous foreign influence into an important part of the
Greek world.

policy which would have won for her the respect and
confidence of many of the Greeks, and might have had
the effect of excluding the intrusion of a most dangerous foreign influence into an important part of the
Greek world.

CHAPTER VI.

FIRST SPEECH OF DEMOSTHENES AGAINST PHILIP—SPEECH FOR THE FREEDOM OF THE PEOPLE OF RHODES.

THE year 352 B.C. brought with it the beginnings of
great events. In that year, for the first time, the king
of Macedon really showed that he might possibly be
entertaining designs fraught with peril to the Greek
world. He had prominently intervened in Greek
politics. He had taken a conspicuous part in the
Sacred or Holy War between the Thebans and Phocians.
Once, indeed, he had been utterly defeated by the
Phocian leader, Onomarchus, and had been driven
back into his kingdom with loss and disaster, though
report made him say that "he did not fly, but fell
back, like the battering-ram, to give a more violent
shock another time." He speedily again entered Thessaly with a more powerful army; and with the help of
his allies in that country and of the admirable Thes-
salian cavalry, he won at Pagasæ a decisive victory
over Onomarchus, who perished in the flight. Now
he was completely master of Thessaly, a country which
ought to have been under the control of a Greek state,
and in which, of late, Theban influence had been

supreme. Macedon was thus in effect the principal
land power to the north of the Peloponnese; and her
king had both displayed military genius, and had
shown that he was in command of an army with
which it was already a question whether any single
Greek state could cope. The battle just fought was
on a very considerable scale, and could not have failed
to suggest unpleasant apprehensions to the mind of
every thinking politician. Philip might very possibly
follow up his success with an instant invasion of
northern Greece. He did in fact advance on Thermopylæ; but Athens had forestalled him, and the
famous pass was guarded by a force before which he
thought it prudent to retire. The Athenians exulted
in the reflection that they had once again been the
deliverers of Greece. But their joy was doomed to be
of very brief duration.

For a few months the king of Macedon employed
himself in securing a firm hold on Thessaly. Meanwhile his cruisers and privateers, of which he had
contrived to raise a formidable number, infested the
northern islands and coasts of the Ægean, to the great
annoyance and injury of Athenian trade. In the
autumn of 352 B.C. he hurried northwards, entered
Thrace, and took advantage of its intestine feuds, with
a view to getting the country under his control. In
November news reached Athens, the serious import of
which could not be misunderstood. Philip was be-
sieging Heræum—a place probably on the northern
coast of the Propontis, to the west of Perinthus. It
was contiguous to the Thracian Chersonese, occupied,

as we have seen, by Athenian colonists, and, as it
appears, actually garrisoned by an Athenian force.
The act was thus one of almost open hostility, and
practically equivalent to a declaration of war. But
what made it singularly alarming was, that it was a
most dangerous menace to the Athenian interests on
the north of the Ægean. It meant, in fact, peril to
the corn trade of Athens, and high prices and possibly
famine to the citizens. It showed too, clearly enough,
that Philip, if he could, would rob the city of its most
valuable outlying possessions. Thus the eyes of the
people ought to have been thoroughly opened to the
danger which hung over them; but as soon as they
knew that Philip was ill, and next heard a report of
his death, they fell back into their love of the easy,
comfortable life at Athens, with its pleasures and
amusements, and flattered themselves with the notion
that the crisis was finally past. The peace party, with
Eubulus at its head, always strong, was now for the
moment stronger than ever; and its best representative,
the really patriotic Phocion, was too cynical to believe
in the possibility of his countrymen being roused to
the degree of effort and endurance which a serious
struggle with Macedon would demand from them.

As soon as it was known that Philip had recovered,
and was as active and aggressive as ever, there were, it
appears, several acrimonious debates in the Assembly,
with grievous complaints as to the inefficiency of the
generals and of their troops. Athens still clung to her
maritime supremacy, and it was felt to be disgraceful
that this should be threatened by a barbarian. Still,

her public men had not the moral courage to tell the people plainly the only way by which such a disgrace could be ended. It was painful to speak to them of personal service on shipboard, with all its hardships and risks. Demosthenes, in his speech on the war with Persia, had hinted, not obscurely, at this necessity. He did so far more clearly and persistently on the occasion we have been describing. At the age of about thirty he spoke the memorable harangue known as the First Philippic.

The speech shows that he had now quite made up his mind on the subject of the foreign policy of Athens. A year ago he had not, as we may reasonably infer, regarded Macedon as a source of real danger to the freedom of the Greek world. He was now convinced that Philip had designs beyond the mere establishment of a compact and powerful northern kingdom. He takes a broad view of the political situation, and speaks not merely as a citizen of the foremost state of Greece, but as a Greek on behalf of Greek security and independence.

It was assuredly much to the honour of Demosthenes that, as a young politician, he sounded a distinct note of warning, which he must have known would have jarred on the easy-going temper of his countrymen. Their affairs, he plainly tells them, were in a very bad plight; but there was hope, just because they had not as yet really exerted themselves. Therefore there was no reason for despair. Philip's power, indeed, was already great: he had Thessaly at his feet; he had defeated a Greek army under a brave and experienced leader; he was now threatening the Chersonese and the northern coasts of the Ægean, and with his fleet was harassing the commerce of Athens; still, he was not a more formidable foe than Sparta had been; and the fact that he was formidable at all was due to their own voluntary supineness, which, for the sake of Greece and for the glory of Athens, they must shake off once and for ever. Otherwise, even if rumour had truly asserted Philip's death, they would soon raise up against themselves another Philip equally terrible.

"You must not despond," he says at the beginning of his speech, "under your present circumstances, wretched as they are; for that which is worst in them as regards the past, is best for the future. My meaning is this—your affairs are amiss because you do nothing which is required. If the result were the same, although you performed your duties, there would be no hope of amendment. Consider, further, what is known to you by hearsay, and what men of experience remember. Not long ago, how vast a power the Lacedæmonians possessed! Yet how nobly and admirably did you consult the dignity of Athens, and undertook the war against them for the rights of Greece! Why do I mention this? To show and convince you that nothing, if you take precaution, is to be feared; nothing, if you are negligent, goes as you desire. Take, for examples, the strength of the Lacedæmonians, which you overcame by minding your duty; and the insolent ambition of this Philip now, which utterly confounds us through our neglect of our interest. If any of you

think the man a formidable foe, looking at the vastness
of his present power and our loss of all our strongholds,
that is reasonable enough; only you should reflect that
there was a time when we held Pydna, and Potidæa,
and Methone, with all the adjacent country, and that
many of the nations now in league with Philip were
independent and free, and preferred our friendship to
his. Had Philip then taken it into his head that
Athens was too formidable a foe to fight, when she
had so many fortresses to threaten his country, and he
was destitute of allies, nothing that he has accomplished
would he have attempted, and never would he have
acquired so large a dominion. But he saw clearly
enough that such places are the open prizes of war ;—
that the possessions of the absent belong to the present, those of the careless to the adventurous who
shrink not from toil. Acting on that principle, he has
won everything, and keeps it either by way of conquest or by friendly attachment and alliance ; for all
men will side with and respect those whom they see
prepared and willing to make proper exertions. If
you will adopt this principle now, though you have
not hitherto done so—and if every man, when he can
and ought to give his service to the State, be ready to
give it without excuse—if the rich will contribute, if
the able-bodied will enlist,—in a word, plainly, if you
will become your own masters, and cease each expecting to do nothing himself, while his neighbour does
everything for him, — then will you, with heaven's
permission, recover your own, and get back what has
been frittered away, and chastise Philip. Do not im-

agine that his empire is everlastingly secured to him as
to a god. There are who hate and fear and envy him,
even among those that seem most friendly; and all
feelings natural to other men exist, we may assume, in
his confederates. But now they are all cowed, for they
have no refuge because of your tardiness and indolence,
which I say you must abandon forthwith."

On the subject of the preparations they ought to
make, Demosthenes thus advises them :—

"First, we must provide fifty war-ships, and hold
ourselves prepared in case of emergency to embark and
sail. There must, too, be an equipment of transports
for half the cavalry, and sufficient boats. This we
must have in readiness against his sudden marches
from his own country to Thermopylæ, the Chersonese,
Olynthus, and anywhere he likes. For he should be
made to have the idea that possibly you may rouse
yourselves out of this over-supineness and start off as
you did to Eubœa, and very lately to Thermopylæ.
Such an armament, I say, ought instantly to be agreed
upon and provided."

In the following passage, the want of skill and
method with which Athens was carrying on the contest is strikingly exposed :—

"You, Athenians, with larger means than any people,
have never up to this day made proper use of any of
them, and your war with Philip is exactly like the
boxing of barbarians. With them, the party struck
first is always feeling for the blow; strike him any-

where else, there go his hands again; ward or look
you in the face he cannot and will not. So with you.
If you hear of Philip in the Chersonese or at Thermopylæ, you vote to send a force there; if you hear of
him somewhere else, you run, so to say, after his heels
up and down, and are, in fact, commanded by him.
No plan have you devised for the war; no circum-
stance do you see beforehand, but only when you learn
that something is done or is about to be done. Formerly, perhaps, this was allowable; now it is come to
a crisis to be borne no longer. It seems as if some
god, in shame at our proceedings, had put this activity
into Philip. For had he been willing to remain quiet
in possession of his conquests and prizes, and attempted
nothing further, some of you, I think, would be satis-
fied with a state of things which brands our nation
with the shame of cowardice and of the foulest disgrace. But by continually encroaching and grasping
after more, he may possibly rouse you, if you have not
altogether despaired. I marvel, indeed, that not one
of you notices with concern and anger that the beginning of this war was to chastise Philip; the end is to
protect ourselves against his attacks."

Towards the conclusion of his speech, Demosthenes
reproaches the people with their silly fondness for
gossiping about Philip's reported movements, and bids
them remember that he now is and long has been their
enemy :—

"Some among ourselves go about and say that
Philip is concerting with the Lacedæmonians the de-

struction of Thebes and the dissolution of free states; some, that he has sent envoys to the King;* others, that he is fortifying cities in Illyria. So we wander about, each inventing stories. For my part, I quite believe that Philip is thoroughly intoxicated with the magnitude of his exploits, and that he has many such dreams in his imagination. Still, most assuredly his plan of action is not such as to let the greatest fools among us know what his intentions are. For the greatest fools are these newsmongers. Let us dismiss such talk, and remember only that Philip is an enemy who robs us of our own, and has long insulted us; that whenever we have expected aid from any quarter, it has been found hostile; and that the future depends on ourselves; and, unless we are willing to fight him there, we shall perhaps be compelled to fight here. This let us remember, and then we shall have determined wisely, and have done with idle conjectures. You need not pry into the future, but assure yourselves that it will be disastrous, unless you give your mind to your duty, and are willing to act as becomes you."

The only result of this speech was, that a paltry four or five ships were sent to the Chersonese under a mercenary and somewhat disreputable general, Charidemus. The fact was, that there was a numerous party at Athens who never could be persuaded that Philip would some day be a really dangerous enemy. Persia was the power of which they were always thinking as

* The king of Persia.

the great source of peril to Greece. There were still rumours flying about as to the gigantic preparations which the King was said to be making against them to revenge the defeats of Marathon and Salamis. Possibly such reports were stimulated by Philip himself. Next there were those who were, in fact, Philip's paid agents, now, no doubt, a considerable class in several Greek states. And, last of all, there was incredulity and apathy among the Athenians themselves. All these adverse influences were too strong for Demosthenes, and his appeal to the patriotism of his countrymen was made in vain.

In the speech we have been describing, Demosthenes dwelt on the duty of Athens to put herself forward as the champion of Greece and of its free states. In a speech delivered some months or perhaps a year afterwards, he reminds her that she ought to be the champion of democracy and of popular government. From this point of view, the oration entitled " On the freedom of the people of Rhodes " has much interest. We rather gather, from the general tone of the speech, that Philip's restlessness had ceased for a time, or at all events that he had something else to do than to threaten the possessions and the commerce of Athens. It was made on the occasion of a deputation from the democratic party in Rhodes, who wished the island to pass again under Athenian control.

Rhodes had more than once been in alliance with Athens—a connection which practically implied a certain degree of subjection and dependence. With the close of the Peloponnesian War and the triumph of

Sparta, it was put under an oligarchy, which meant
Spartan control. About the year 396 B.C. the Athenian
general Conon, who had a powerful fleet in the Ægean,
again forced the Rhodians to become the allies of
Athens. Four years afterwards a Spartan fleet appeared,
and this was the signal for another revolution in the
government. There was, it seems, one of those horrible
incidents with which Greek history is so often dis-
figured—a massacre of the democratic leaders and of
the adherents of Athens. But the oligarchy now imposed on the island did not last long. The Spartan
fleet was defeated, and Rhodes and most of the islands
of the Ægean returned to the Athenian alliance. We
may take for granted that democracy was re-established.
Then came, in 358 B.C., the Social War, the war between
Athens and her allies, which broke up the second
Athenian empire. Of this, Rhodes was the orig n.
Chares, the Athenian general, of whom we have
already had occasion to speak, provoked and disgusted
the Rhodians by plunder and extortion. Cos and
Chios had similar grievances ; and the three islands
threw off their connection with Athens, and began the
Social War—Rhodes being the prime mover. They
were helped by Mausolus, king of Caria and a vassal
prince of the Persian empire. He was a man of considerable ambition, and his idea was to annex Rhodes,
which was adjacent to his own territories. It was first
necessary to detach it from the Athenian alliance ; and
Mausolus contrived, by intrigues with the oligarchical
party in the island, to introduce a Carian garrison ; and
once more the government was revolutionised. The

people and their leaders found themselves in a hopeless plight, now that they had renounced their connection with Athens, while the oligarchy was supported by Persian influence through Mausolus. When that king died and his queen Artemisia succeeded, the government became so intolerably oppressive that the popular party ventured to send an embassy to Athens, and humbly to implore relief. It was hardly to be expected that the embassy would be well received. The Athenians felt that Rhodes had inflicted a grievous injury on them by plunging them in a disastrous war, which had ended in dissolving their confederacy. They were in no mood to listen to the present petition. Nevertheless it was supported by Demosthenes.

It is a hard matter to soothe the temper of people when they feel, as the Athenians now did, that they have suffered much from ingratitude. Popular assemblies, under such circumstances, are apt to be peculiarly angry and excited. All that Demosthenes could do was to appeal to the better and more generous sentiments of his countrymen. They ought not, he argued, to brood over the wrongs done to them by these insignificant islanders, but to think only of what was due to Athens and to Greece. It was alike their duty and interest to vindicate the freedom of an oppressed Greek people, and to stand by the policy of supporting popular and democratic government against oligarchs and tyrants. Unless they resolved to act thus, the political constitution of Athens would itself be imperilled. If all democracies were put down, their own would fall at last. Demosthenes, we see, was heartily in sympathy with democracy, and regarded it as the special glory of Athens to be its champion and upholder. If at times he felt its weak side, and its tendency to vacillation and irresolution, still he never seems to have doubted that it was on the whole the best and most manly type of government.

Such were his reasons for counselling the assembly to listen favourably to the request for aid from the Rhodians. In the following passage these views are clearly expressed :—

"Observe, men of Athens, that you have waged many wars both against democracies and against oligarchies. This you know without my telling; but for what causes you have been at war with either, perhaps not one of you considers. What are the causes? Against democratical states your wars have been either for private grievances, when you could not make public satisfaction, or for territory or boundaries, or a point of honour, or for the leadership of Greece. Against oligarchies you fought, not for such things, but for your constitution and for freedom. Therefore I would not hesitate to say that I think it better that all the Greeks should be your enemies with a popular government than your friends under an oligarchical. For with free men I consider you would have no difficulty in making peace when you chose; but with people under an oligarchy, even friendship I hold to be insecure. It is impossible that the few can be attached to the many, the seekers of power to the lovers of constitutional equality. I marvel none of you consider that, when the Rhodians and nearly all people are drawn into this slavery, our constitution must be in the same peril. If all other governments are oligarchical, it is impossible that they will let your democracy alone. They know too well that no other people will bring things back to freedom; therefore they will wish to destroy a government from which they apprehend mischief to themselves. Ordinary wrong-doers you may regard as enemies to the sufferers; while they who subvert constitutions and transform them into oligarchies must be looked upon as the common enemies of all lovers of freedom."

In the opinion of Demosthenes it thus appears that oligarchy was in fact slavery, and wholly alien to the Greek genius. The memory of the Athens of Pericles was deeply impressed on his mind. But he felt he was now addressing a people singularly prone to be misled. He hints plainly in this speech at the existence of an unpatriotic faction in the State.

"It is difficult for you," he says, "to adopt right measures. All other men have one battle to fight—namely, against their open and avowed enemies. You have a double contest—that which the rest have, and also a prior and a more arduous one. You must in counsel overcome a faction which acts among you in systematic opposition to the State. Men who desert the politics handed down to them by their ancestors, and support oligarchical measures, should be degraded and deprived of constitutional privileges, and disqualified from being your political advisers."

Again Demosthenes failed. The bitterness of Athenian feeling towards the ungrateful islanders made the people blind to higher considerations, and Rhodes remained in the hands of an oligarchy. It was still subject to Caria, and was thus really a Persian dependency.

CHAPTER VII.

PHILIP AND OLYNTHUS—SPEECHES OF DEMOSTHENES ON BEHALF OF THE OLYNTHIANS.

WHEN Demosthenes, some time in the year 352 B.C., made his first speech against Philip, there were good grounds for an uneasy feeling throughout the Greek world as to the king's possible movements and designs. He had already raised Macedon to a position it had never before held. It had become a distinct power in the politics of Greece. For a while, however, the usually active Philip seemed to be really resting from his labours, and next to nothing was heard of him. Demosthenes does not so much as allude to him in his speech "for the freedom of the people of Rhodes." We may fairly infer from his silence that anything like serious apprehensions at Athens of peril from "the barbarian," as Philip was called, had died away. The peace party, always strong, and able to make out a plausible case for itself, would thus be strengthened; and it would not be easy, even in the face of manifest danger, thoroughly to rouse the Athenians to a sense of the duty which they owed both to themselves and to Greece.

Philip was by this time a powerful prince; but still he was as yet barely a match for Athens, had she chosen to put forth her full strength. He had an efficient army and a good revenue, and he also had the luck to have other collateral advantages. He had tools and agents in several Greek states; and he had practically on his side at Athens very many of the rich and well-to-do citizens, who shrank from the idea of a war which required personal service and exertion. It was perfectly clear that a contest with him would have been a serious undertaking. At the same time, his position, though strong, was not altogether secure. He had, as we have seen, possessed himself of some of the coast towns, and he had a fleet in the Ægean. Athens should never have allowed him to advance to this point. She had flung away opportunities; but even now it was not too late to check him with the help of a seasonable alliance. As yet he had no hold on the district known as Chalcidice, which juts out with its three peninsulas into the north-west of the Ægean. It was a valuable and commanding strip of country; and it contained thirty Greek towns, of which the chief was the city Olynthus, at the head of the Toronæan gulf. Some of these towns regarded themselves as dependencies of Olynthus, and formed what was known as the Olynthian confederacy. There was a time when even Pella, now the capital of Macedonia, was included in their number. Olynthus, indeed, had been quite the most powerful city in the north of the Ægean, and far too proud to submit to the supremacy of either Sparta or

Athens. Sparta with much difficulty forced it, in 379 B.C., into the Lacedæmonian confederacy; and Athens, about ten years later, very much weakened its influence by taking from it some of its territory and of its subject-towns. Still, however, it was prosperous and flourishing; and it could, at an extremity, bring into the field a considerable military force, especially of cavalry. Although it owed Athens a grudge, it had, as we have seen, proposed alliance when it saw its neighbour, Amphipolis, pass into the hands of Philip. Athens declined the offer, and Philip was clever enough temporarily to conciliate the goodwill of the Olynthians by a trifling concession of territory,—intending, no doubt, at the first convenient moment, to pick a quarrel with them and annex the whole district. It must have been easy for him, in the case of a city immediately in his own neighbourhood, to have his partisans among the citizens; and it was to this that he was indebted for his ultimate success. The towns, too, which were connected with Olynthus by the loose tie of federation, were no doubt singularly open to his intrigues. Still, there was the feeling that he might become a dangerous aggressor; and accordingly Olynthus decided on a change of policy, and, in 352 B.C., withdrew itself from the Macedonian alliance. The next step was to conclude peace with Athens, and even to show a wish for a yet closer union with that state. Athens, too, now saw the advantage of such a union, and, indeed, actually made overtures to that effect; but Olynthus was not quite prepared to commit itself definitely to an Athenian alliance, which it well knew would be equivalent to a declaration of hostility against Philip.

Before long, however,—in the year B.C. 350, as it seems,—Philip left the Olynthians no alternative but that of seeking powerful support. He made them feel that they were in imminent danger by a sudden and unprovoked attack on one of those cities of Chalcidice which would naturally look to Olynthus for sympathy and protection. Their eyes were now completely opened, and they instantly sent off an embassy to Athens. Philip, indeed, tried to persuade them by envoys that he had no intention of making war on them; but he could not blind them. They felt sure that they might count on a favourable reception for their envoys at Athens, and on the prospect of assistance. Nor were they disappointed. It was impossible for the Athenians to neglect such an opportunity. They had themselves lately proposed such an alliance, and now it was offered them. There could be no mistake as to the critical nature of the situation. Philip had attacked and taken a Greek city, and it was hardly possible to doubt that he was feeling his way to the conquest and annexation of the entire peninsula of Chalcidice, with its thirty towns. Were he to be successful, it was clear that his power would be immensely increased. Equally clear was it that Olynthus, if well supported, might effectually stop his further progress. Indeed, so sanguine were the Athenians, that the general talk now was about punishing Philip for his perfidy. Only one statesman and orator of any note, Demades, who was rarely to be found on the patriotic side, and was subsequently in all probability a mere creature of Philip's, spoke against the proposed alliance.

It was on this occasion that Demosthenes, in the latter half probably of the year 350 B.C., delivered three memorable speeches, commonly known as the "Olynthiacs." He must have felt that the convictions of the people were with him; and yet at the same time he lets us see, by his general tone, that he almost despaired of being able to stir them to decisive action. All that they could be persuaded to do was to send thirty galleys and 2000 mercenaries. This poor little force could not stop Philip from continuing his attacks on the Greek towns of Chalcidice. He had not yet entered Olynthian territory, or even declared war against the city; but Olynthus was sufficiently alarmed to send a second embassy to Athens, begging for more effectual help. A large force was now despatched; but it consisted of mercenaries, and, unfortunately for Athens, it was under the command of a man who, though he had some military talent, was so disreputable in his life that he utterly disgusted the Olynthians.

In the speech which was probably first delivered, Demosthenes seeks to encourage his countrymen to take a hopeful view of affairs by pointing out to them how it really was that Philip had risen to power, and how numerous were the elements of weakness in his kingdom and government.

" He has risen by conciliating and cajoling the simplicity of every people which knew him not. When one has grown strong, as he has, by rapacity and artifice, on the first pretext, the slightest reason, all is overturned and broken up. If you will perform your duties properly, not only will it appear that Philip's alliances are weak and precarious, but the poor state of his native empire and power will be revealed. To speak roundly, the Macedonian power is very well as a help, as it was for you in the time of Timotheus against the Olynthians. For them, too, against Potidæa, it was an important alliance. Lately, as you know, it aided the Thessalians in their broils and troubles against the regnant house; and indeed the accession of any power, however small, is undoubtedly useful. But of itself Macedon is feeble, and has numberless deficiencies. The very operations which seem to constitute Philip's greatness—his wars and his expeditions—have made it more insecure than it was originally. Do not imagine that Philip and his subjects have the same likings. He craves glory—makes that his passion; is ready for any consequence of adventure and peril—preferring, as he does, to a life of safety, the honour of achieving what no Macedonian king ever did before. They have no share in the glorious result: ever harassed by these excursions, they suffer and toil without ceasing; they have no leisure for their employments or private affairs, and cannot so much as dispose of their hard earnings, the markets of the country being closed on account of the war. We may easily infer from all this what is the general Macedonian feeling towards Philip. His mercenaries and guards, indeed, have the reputation of admirable and well-trained soldiers; but, as I heard from one who had been born in the country, they are no better than others. If some of them are experienced in battles and campaigns, Philip is jealous of such men, and drives them away— so my informant tells me—wishing to keep the glory of all action to himself. Or again, if a man is generally good and virtuous, unable to bear Philip's daily intemperance, drunkenness, and indecency, he is pushed aside and accounted as nobody. The rest about him are brigands and parasites, and men of that character who will get drunk and perform dances which I scruple to name before you. My information is undoubtedly true; for persons whom all scouted here as worse rascals than mountebanks,—Callias, the town-slave, and the like of him—antic-jesters and composers of ribald songs to lampoon their companions,—such persons Philip caresses and keeps about him. Small matters these may be thought, but to the wise they are strong indications of his character and wrongheadedness. Success perhaps throws a shade over them now; prosperity is a famous hider of such blemishes; but on any miscarriage they will be fully exposed."

Though in the above passage Demosthenes speaks contemptuously of Philip, describing him as little better than a savage and barbarian, he warns his hearers that if they let Olynthus fall into his hands, he will soon carry the war into Attica itself. The third and last of his three speeches was delivered when the Olynthians entreated Athens to send out a force of her own

citizens, instead of mercenaries commanded by men of
the type of the officer whose misconduct, as we have
seen, had given them so much offence. Of all the
political orations of Demosthenes, this is perhaps the
most stirring and impressive. It is, in the opinion of
Mr Grote, one of the most splendid harangues ever
spoken. It seems that people at Athens still talked
about punishing Philip; and there were orators, no
doubt, who flattered them into the notion that they
could do so whenever they chose. "Such talk," says
Demosthenes, "is founded on a false basis. The facts
of the case teach us a different lesson. They bid us
look well to our own security, that we be not ourselves
the sufferers, and that we preserve our allies. There
was, indeed, a time—and that, too, within my own
remembrance—when we might have held our own, and
punished Philip besides; but now our first care must be
to preserve our own allies." In this speech he ventures
on a bold proposal, which would be sure to provoke
bitter opposition from the peace party of Eubulus.
"Repeal such of the existing laws as are injurious at
the present crisis—I mean those which regard the public
entertainments fund. I speak this out plainly. The
same men who proposed such a law ought also to take
upon them to propose its repeal." In speaking thus,
Demosthenes knew that he was fighting against a most
powerful Athenian sentiment. It would cost them a
painful struggle to sacrifice the fund in question to the
exigencies of a war which also demanded personal
service. They could hardly become like the men who
won Marathon and Salamis. There was the broadest

contrast between them, as Demosthenes elaborately points out in the following passage :—

"Mark, Athenians, what a summary contrast may be drawn between the doings in our olden time and in yours. It is a tale brief and familiar to all. Our forefathers for forty-five years took the leadership of Greece by general consent, and brought as much as ten thousand talents into the citadel; and the king of Macedonia was submissive to them, as a barbarian should be to Greeks. Many glorious trophies they erected for victories won by their own fighting on land and sea, and they are the sole people in the world who have bequeathed a renown which envy cannot hurt. Such were their merits in the affairs of Greece; now see what they were at home, both as citizens and men. Their public works are edifices and ornaments of such beauty and grandeur in temples and their consecrated furniture, that posterity has not the power to surpass them. In private they were so modest, and so attached to the principles of our constitution, that whoever knows the style of house which Aristides had or Miltiades, and the illustrious of that day, perceives it to be no grander than those of their neighbours. Their politics were not for money-making; each felt it his duty to exalt the commonwealth. By a conduct honourable among the Greeks, pious to the gods, brotherlike among themselves, they justly attained a high prosperity.

"So fared matters with them under the statesmen I have named. How fare they with you under the worthies of our time? Is there any likeness or resemblance? I pass over other topics on which I could expatiate. But observe. In the utter absence of competitors (Lacedæmonians depressed, Thebans employed, none of the rest capable of disputing the supremacy with us), when we might hold our own securely and arbitrate the claims of others, we have been deprived of our rightful territory, and spent above 1500 talents to no purpose. The allies whom we gained in war we have lost in peace, and we have trained up against ourselves an enemy thus formidable. For by whose contrivance but our own has Philip grown strong? This looks bad, you will say, but things at home are better. What proof is there of this? The parapets that are whitewashed, the roads that are repaired, the fountains, and such trumpery things? Look at the men of whose statesmanship these are the fruits. They have risen from beggary to opulence, from obscurity to honour. Some have made their private homes more splendid than the public buildings, and as the State has declined, their fortunes have been exalted."

At last Athens roused herself to a real effort, and sent to the relief of her ally a force of more than 2000 native Athenian citzens. Olynthus might yet have been saved had the Olynthians been on their guard against traitors within, and the history of Greece, perhaps of the world, might have been different. Philip, meanwhile, was on the frontier of its territory, after having captured most of the towns in the peninsula. At the siege of one of them, an arrow from an Olynthian archer deprived him of an eye. But early in the year 348 B.C. he attacked Olynthus itself, after a sudden declaration of war. The Olynthians, he said, must quit their city, or he must quit Macedonia. But he did not overcome them by fair fighting. They were betrayed by a party among their fellow-citizens. It was by bribery, as Horace says,* that "the man of Macedon" opened the gates of Olynthus as of other cities. It was to be expected that he would show no mercy. The fair city was razed to the ground, and its population, with all the women and children, sold into slavery.

This awful calamity sent a shudder through the Greek world. The like of it had never been seen since the great Persian invasion of Xerxes. As many as thirty-two free Greek cities had utterly perished in a period of less than two years at the hands of a bar-barian. Divided as the Greeks were among themselves, they would have all heartily responded to the sentiment of Demosthenes that "a barbarian should be submissive to Greeks." It must have shocked and shamed them to see with their own eyes troops of poor enslaved crea-tures, of both sexes and of Greek blood, passing through the streets of their cities. And all this was the work of a Macedonian, a man of inferior race, whom Greeks had thought it almost a condescension to notice and patron-ise. How could they expect that he would much longer stay his hand from the destruction of the Greek cities on the Hellespont and the Propontis, and from the conquest of the rich corn-producing Chersonese? How

* Odes, iii. 16, 13.

could they rest in peace till they saw their way to an
alliance of all the states of Greece against him? It is
natural for us to reason thus. But even the proximity
of manifest danger will not always banish mutual
jealousy and distrust. Nor is it in general easy to persuade people that a power they have been accustomed
to disregard and despise, though its progress may
seem at times alarming, can ever become seriously
formidable to themselves. So it appears to have been
with the Greeks. After the fall of Olynthus and its
confederate cities, they still clung to their false confidence.

CHAPTER VIII.

DEMOSTHENES AND MEIDIAS.

An incident about this time in the life of Demosthenes, which gave occasion to one of his well-known speeches, illustrates rather strikingly some of the less agreeable phases of Athenian society. There was, of course, refinement and polish of a high degree, and, on the whole, the tone and temper of the citizens seem to have been humane and generous. But still, even at Athens, the scandals and breaches of good taste and manners, which one would fear are all but inseparable from democracy, now and then made their appearance. Political rancour and party violence reached an outrageous length, and under their shelter the grossest acts of wrong were from time to time committed with impunity. A rich man, if he chose, might have plenty of influence in the State; and along with this he would have at his command many opportunities of injuring and oppressing those whom he personally disliked. It appears that there were several such men at Athens—men who no doubt aspired to imitate the grand airs and fashionable extravagance of Alcibiades, who, clever and accomplished as he was, at last made himself intolerable to the citi-

zens of a free state. Many of these had nothing but
riches to recommend them, and were pestilent fellows
whose idea of life was really nothing better than coarse,
vulgar rowdyism.

It was the fate of Demosthenes to come into collision
with a man of this class. Early in life, at the time
when he was engaged in his suit with his guardians,
he provoked the enmity of Meidias, a rich, well-born
man, and one of the constant supporters of the peace
party of Eubulus. The quarrel between them originated
in the following singular way. The brother of Meidias,
Thrasylochus, offered, according to a practice allowed
at Athens in the case of a trierarchy, or the providing a war-ship for the State, to exchange properties
with Demosthenes, and, in the event of the offer being
accepted, he gave the guardians privately to understand
that the lawsuit should be dropped. In this manner
he sought to defeat the legal proceedings which Demosthenes was taking, and, in fact, to get his just claims
set aside. The two brothers, it appears, on one occasion
actually rushed into his house, behaved with excessive
violence, and used coarse and ribald language in the
presence of his sister, then a mere girl. For this outrage
Demosthenes sued Meidias, and recovered damages; but
he had not been able to obtain payment. From that
time the man became his bitter enemy, and worried and
persecuted him in every possible way. His animosity
was all the more virulent as he was also politically
opposed to Demosthenes. In the year 351 B.C. both
served in a military expedition to Eubœa—Meidias in
the cavalry, Demosthenes as a foot soldier. Neither

of them was for any length of time with the army. Demosthenes went back to Athens, on the pretext that he had to undertake the important public duty of choragus or choir-director for his tribe. It seems that he undertook this quite voluntarily, but his enemy hinted that he had merely done so to escape the hardships of campaigning. And he followed up the taunt with gross insult and outrage. The choir-director, as we have seen, usually appeared, when the ceremony was celebrated, in a special dress, and wore a crown; and Demosthenes had ordered for the occasion a particularly magnificent robe and a crown of gold. Meidias contrived to break into the embroiderer's shop where the dress had been prepared, and spoilt the finery in which Demosthenes was to show himself. He went further; he struck him on the face before the assembled audience, and, according to Demosthenes' own account, was the means of losing him the prize, which his chorus would have won. The spectators were indignant; and Meidias was convicted of the crime of sacrilege, as it would seem, on the very same day by an assembly held in the theatre. But the affair could not rest here. It was for a court of justice to decide how he was to be punished. Clearly, it was right that Demosthenes should prosecute him, and this he did. He was thirty-two years of age at the time. Meidias tried to defeat the prosecution by indicting Demosthenes on the charge of desertion of military service, on the ground that he had left the army in Eubœa and returned to Athens. The indictment came to nothing; but Demosthenes, it appears, was not decisively successful in his proceedings against Meidias. He was reproached by his rival, Æschines, with having compromised the affair. At all events, it is not certain whether the case was ever brought to trial. But the tone of the extant speech certainly implies this; and it is really difficult to suppose, looking at some passages in which he takes credit to himself for having rejected a compromise and having brought the defendant to trial, that it was merely written and never delivered. This is, we know, a very general opinion, and there are reasons for it; but in the face of the speech as it has come down to us, it seems a question whether it can be sustained.

The tone of the speech is savage and violent. It is full of furious invective. But at least it is interesting as giving us a glimpse into some of the abuses arising out of wealth and insolence even in a democratical community like Athens. We have an amusing picture of Meidias himself; and though perhaps it is a caricature, it was no doubt typical of a really existing class. He had, it is said, got himself elected a cavalry officer on the strength of being a rich man, and yet he could not so much as ride through the market-place. His single act of munificence was giving the State a war-ship, when he knew he was not likely to incur any personal danger. He delighted in making a vulgar parade of his wealth. He had built a house at Eleusis, one of the suburbs of Athens, so big that it darkened all the houses in the place. He used to take his wife to the Mysteries, or to any place she had a fancy for visiting, in a carriage and pair. He would push through the market-place and the leading thoroughfares, talking of his dinners and his drinking-horns so loud that all the passers-by could hear. "Do not," says Demosthenes in his speech, "honour and admire things of this kind—do not judge of liberality by these tests, whether a man builds splendid houses or has many female servants, or handsome furniture; but look who is spirited and liberal in those things which the bulk of you share the enjoyment of. Meidias, you will find, has nothing of that kind about him."

"Will you," he asks, "let Meidias escape because he is rich? This is pretty much the cause of his insolence. Therefore you should rather take away the means which enable him to be insolent than pardon him in consideration of them. To allow an audacious blackguard like him to have wealth at his command is to put arms in his hands against yourselves."

"I take it you all know his disposition, his offensive and overbearing behaviour; and some of you, I daresay, have been wondering about things which they know themselves, but have not heard from me now. Many of the injured parties do not even like to tell all that they have suffered, dreading this man's litigiousness, and the fortune which makes such a despicable fellow strong and terrible. For when a rogue and a bully is supported by wealth and power, it is a wall of defence against any attack. Let Meidias be stripped of his possessions, and most likely he will not play the bully. If he should, he will be less regarded than the humblest man among you; he will rail and bawl to no purpose then, and be punished for any misbehaviour like the rest of us. Now, it seems, Polyeuctus and Timocrates and the ragamuffin Euctemon are his body-guard; these are a sort of mercenaries that he keeps about him, and others also besides them, a confederate band of witnesses, who never trouble you openly, but by simply nodding their heads affirm and lie with perfect ease. By the powers, I do not believe they get any good from him; but they are wonderful people for making up to the rich, and attending on them, and giving evidence. All this, I take it, is a danger to any of you that live quietly by yourselves as well as you can; and therefore it is that you assemble together, in order that, though taken separately you are over-matched by any one either in friends or riches, or in anything else, you may collectively be more than a match for him and put a stop to his insolence."

Meidias, according to Demosthenes, was at heart a coward, and would be sure to make an abject appeal to the people's pity. The following passage is towards the end of the speech :—

"I know he will have his children in court and whine; he will talk very humbly, shedding tears and making himself as piteous as he can. Yet the more he humbles himself, the more ought you to detest him. Why? Because if the outrageousness and violence of his conduct arose out of his inability to be humble, it would have been fair to make some allowance for his temper, and the accident which made him what he is. But if he knows how to behave himself properly when he likes, and has adopted a different line of conduct by choice, surely it is quite evident that if he eludes justice now, he will again become the same Meidias that you know him for. You must not listen to him, then; you must not let the present occasion, when he is playing the hypocrite, have more weight and influence with you than the whole past of which you have had experience.

"Perhaps he will say of me, This man is an orator. Well; if one who advises what he thinks for your good, without being troublesome or intrusive, is an orator, I would not deny or refuse the name. But if an orator be what (to my knowledge and to your knowledge) certain of our speakers are—impudent fellows, enriched at your expense—I can hardly be that; for I have received nothing from you, but spent all my substance upon you, except a mere trifle. Probably, also, Meidias will say that all my speech is prepared. I admit that I have got it up as well as I possibly could. I were a complete simpleton indeed, if, having suffered and still suffering such injuries, I took no pains about the mode of stating them to you. I maintain that Meidias has composed my speech; he who has supplied the facts which the speech is about, may most fairly be deemed its author, not he who has merely prepared it or studied how to lay an honest case before you."

The speech is not, we think, one of Demosthenes' best; but it is often ingenious, and it certainly shows singular power of invective. It suggests that what we

should call very loose practice on the part of an advocate was tolerated in an Athenian court. Demosthenes
by no means confines himself to the outrage committed
on him by Meidias, but speaks of the injuries he had
inflicted on others, and indeed attacks generally the
man's whole life and character. The attack may have
been deserved; still, the manner of it, and the circumstances under which it was made, point to the existence of dangers at Athens to which any citizen might
suddenly find himself exposed.

CHAPTER IX.

WE now enter on a period of melancholy disgrace and
humiliation for the Greek race. Within two years the
barbarian destroyer of Olynthus becomes master of the
key to Greece, the famous pass of Thermopylæ, and of
the whole of Phocis, the country in which stood the
mountains of Parnassus, and the old and venerable
temple of Delphi. Events more terrific and momentous,
says Demosthenes in one of his speeches, had never
occurred either in his own time or in that of any of his
predecessors. Athens was forced into a miserably
ignominious peace, and many of her citizens had
stooped to the infamy of being the mere tools and
paid agents of the "man of Macedon." Even Isocrates,
true Greek as he was in all his sympathies, as well as
thoroughly upright and high-minded, was now convinced that the best wisdom for Greece was to put
itself under the leadership of this wonderfully successful prince, and allow him to conduct its united armies
to the conquest of Persia.

The history of these five years is somewhat intricate. It will be enough for the present purpose to summarise the general course of events. The period was mainly occupied in negotiations on the part of Athens with Philip. These were ill-managed, and had a most disastrous conclusion. One motive which no doubt prompted them was, the very natural desire of recovering those Athenian citizens who had been captured with the Olynthians. Toward Athens Philip had usually shown himself gracious and conciliatory. So, when the relatives of two of the captives, both men of high position, presented themselves as suppliants before the Assembly, it was decided to communicate with Philip. A favourable answer was received ; and we have reason to believe that now there was an inclination in favour of peace. At first it was otherwise. Even Eubulus and his party, who held war the worst of all evils, were constrained to speak of Philip as an enemy. They went further ; they attempted, by embassies into the Peloponnese, to raise some sort of coalition against him. Among other places they visited Megalopolis, where, however, their overtures met with but a cold reception. Athens, as we have had occasion to notice, had made a blunder some years before in not following the counsel of Demosthenes when he advised that the Megalopolitans should be supported against Sparta. Now she found that they were not to be roused into action by what no doubt seemed to them a comparatively remote danger. There would, too, have been some political inconvenience in an alliance with them. Such an alliance would have meant a rupture with Sparta, and a friendly attitude towards Thebes, a state against which Athenian feeling was peculiarly bitter. As soon as it seemed clear that there was no prospect of organising a combination throughout Greece against Philip, the wish for peace grew in strength, and the people were not averse to opening negotiations with their powerful enemy.

It is at this juncture that the name of Demosthenes' famous rival Æschines first comes before us. He rose to be one of the foremost Athenian orators and statesmen from a very lowly origin. His father kept what we should call a preparatory school, and he himself began life as an inferior actor and a government clerk. He was a man of immense industry and ability, and was naturally endowed with all the qualities which go to make an orator. He was one of the envoys sent on the mission to the Peloponnese, which had for its purpose the stirring up of the Greeks against Macedonian aggression. It appears that he addressed a very powerful appeal to the Arcadian Assembly at Megalopolis, fiercely denouncing all traitors to the liberties of Greece, and stigmatising Philip as a "bloodstained barbarian." Such was the beginning of the political life of a man who subsequently allowed himself to become the means of furthering that "barbarian's" most dangerous designs upon Greece and her liberties.

In the negotiations of this period between Athens and Philip, Æschines took a leading part as an envoy. So, too, did Demosthenes himself; and the hostile relations between them, which subsequently gave occasion to their memorable oratorical contest, date from this time. We have for the most part to depend on the conflicting statements of the two orators for our knowledge of the circumstances by which Athens, two years after the ruin of Olynthus, was drawn into a shameful peace. It almost seems as if she wilfully allowed herself to make one stupid blunder after another. But this is not a true view of the case. Athens, no doubt, might have done much better under the guidance of really firm and very skilful statesmanship; but it must be remembered that the situation was extremely complicated, and it was barely possible to foresee even approximately the course and tendency of events. After the destruction of Olynthus it must have seemed clear that Philip was the enemy of Greece; and that, consequently, it was the duty and policy of Athens to regard him in this light, and decline all negotiations with him. But, as we have seen, Athens was not able to organise a confederacy of the Greek states against him; and if she had decided to fight him, she must have felt that she would have to fight single-handed. When to this consideration was added the desire to recover some of her own citizens, now prisoners in Philip's hands—when, too, she found that he was still courteous and conciliatory—we cannot be surprised that she shrank from a struggle which would have tasked her resources to the uttermost. It might, perhaps, have been better and safer for her to have made any sacrifice, and have at once decided on war against the destroyer of thirty Greek cities; but it was not easy for her to see her way to such a step alone and unsupported.

The relations, too, of the states of Greece to each other and to Athens presented many difficulties. Never had there been a time when it was harder to unite them. Sparta, the leading state of the Peloponnese, could under no circumstances be easily stimulated into exertions in the Greek cause. Her statesmen were apt to take a narrow and selfish view of the politics of Greece. The other states of the Peloponnese were more afraid of being oppressed by Spartan ascendancy, of which they had had actual experience, than of danger from Macedon, of which they knew next to nothing. Here, therefore, there was but a poor prospect of coalition. Thebes and Phocis, the two remaining states, were themselves engaged in the Sacred War. Phocis had appropriated to itself the treasures of the temple of Delphi, and had thus put itself in a false position before the Greek world, as being guilty of sacrilege. And as for Thebes, it had no really great and far-sighted statesmen; nor had it, to the extent which Athens still had, a sense of its duty to Greece. Its policy was often particularly selfish; and even under the most favourable circumstances, it would have been most difficult to have persuaded Thebans to co-operate heartily with Athenians. So anxious was it to crush its Phocian neighbours, with whom it had long been involved in a troublesome war, that when Philip undertook to crush them it welcomed the offer. The bait he held out was tempting; but the Thebans ought to have had enough Greek sentiment not to listen to his proposals, the acceptance of which would probably lead to the conquest and destruction of a Greek people by a barbarian. Philip, of course, could justify himself by saying that he was attacking those who were, in fact, the enemies of Greece, inasmuch as by the pillage of the sacred treasures of Delphi they had outraged the best and truest Greek feeling. But to conquer Phocis he must be master of Thermopylæ ; and if he once gained this position, it could hardly be doubted that he would be able to do as he pleased, and that Thebes, if he chose to pick a quarrel with her, would be in the utmost jeopardy.

All this was recognised by Demosthenes, and, as it seems, by the Athenians generally. They were quite alive to the importance of garrisoning Thermopylæ, and they sent a force there. But the Phocian leader, Phalæcus, from some sort of jealousy towards Athens, and a fear that political intrigues would be set on foot against him to deprive him of his influence with his countrymen, refused to admit the Athenian troops into possession of the important pass. It was now difficult for the Athenians to know how to act. For anything they knew to the contrary, Phalæcus might have some understanding with Philip, and be willing to surrender the pass to him. This position was perplexing and disheartening, while to Philip it was a grand opportunity. If he could contrive to conclude peace with Athens, and to get the Phocians excluded from it, he would be able, with some sort of excuse, to occupy Thermopylæ and invade Phocis. And in doing this, he would have Thebes on his side.

After much negotiation, this was the result which he managed to accomplish. Peace was concluded between Philip and Athens, their respective allies being included. While the negotiations were pending, and the Athenian envoys were waiting at Pella for an interview with the King, he was in Thrace, and gained some important successes over the chief of the country, Cersobleptes, at this time an ally of Athens. The effect of this was to weaken and endanger the hold which Athens had on the Thracian Chersonese,—a specially valuable possession. Indeed, peace was made ultimately on terms which the Athenians had not originally contemplated. This, Demosthenes maintained, was due to the treacherous connivance of Æschines and of some of the other envoys, who loitered at Pella when they ought to have at once made their way to Philip in Thrace, and settled matters with him on the basis which had been mutually agreed on. But the most terrible mistake was the exclusion of the Phocians from the treaty. The Athenians were somehow cajoled into believing that Philip meant them well; and even Demosthenes did not at the time protest against the abandonment of Phocis. The error was irretrievable, for it amounted to nothing less than letting Philip become master of Thermopylæ. The Phocians could not hold the pass without support. When they found themselves isolated, their leader, Phalæcus, after being summoned by Philip to give up possession of it, consented to do so under a convention, and withdrew his forces. The surrender of Phocis to Philip followed as a matter of course. He dealt with the country and its towns as he had dealt two years before with Chalcidice and its towns. Phocis was utterly ruined. Another Greek state had now fallen before the Macedonian destroyer, and the prospects of Greece generally might well seem gloomy.

The calamity, however, was not so shocking to the Greek world as one might have supposed it would have been. The Phocians, as has been explained, had been offenders against the common law and traditions of Greece, and their destruction might be regarded as a divine judgment. Even the man who executed it, though a barbarian according to Greek notions, might have some claim to be considered as the representative of a sacred cause. In one sense he had been doing the very thing which the voice of Greece had been calling for. The Thebans were especially grateful to him, and forgot in their blindness the mischief which by this last stroke he had inflicted on Greece. Now that the Phocians had ceased to exist as a Greek people, their place in the Amphictyonic Council was, when the great Pythian festival came round after a four years' interval, conferred on Philip. He was even nominated president of the august ceremony. In all this Thebes heartily concurred, as also did several smaller states. Athens and Sparta, indeed, held aloof. But when Philip's envoys announced to the Athenians the new position he had acquired with the consent of so many Greek states, they did not like to refuse concurrence in what a large part of Greece seemed to approve.

Strong as Philip was before, he was now immensely strengthened, and fresh chances were open to him for interfering actively in Greek politics. Membership of the Amphictyonic Council was, in fact, equivalent to naturalisation. Philip was now, in theory at least, a Greek, and no longer a barbarian. The Athenian Isocrates could, with a show of reason, address a letter to him, inviting him to reconcile under his leadership the great states of Greece, and invade Asia with a view to the overthrow of the Persian empire and the liberation of the Asiatic Greeks. But the Athenians generally felt deep anger and vexation at the issue of events, and could hardly make up their minds to sit still under the disgrace of the surrender of Thermopylæ and the intrusion of a foreign prince into the heart of Greece.

Demosthenes, as has been said, had no sympathy with the ideas of Isocrates. He still clung to the belief in a general independent Greek world, of which his own state ought to be the most perfect representative. Yet on this occasion he spoke in favour of the inglorious peace just concluded. Miserable as it was, he argued that to break it would be to give Philip a pretext for uniting other Greek states in war against them. The tone of his speech is confident and decided. The peace was bad and dishonourable, no doubt, but to repudiate it would be simply madness. It would be putting themselves gratuitously in the wrong. "The shadow at Delphi," as he calls the subject of the Sacred war which had been waged between Thebes and Phocis, was not worth fighting for, more especially when they would have to fight a Greek confederacy. It could not have been altogether pleasant to Demosthenes to advise acquiescence in a peace which he and his countrymen generally felt to be humiliating. But as they had drifted into it, all they could now do was to make the best of it, and guard themselves from new aggressions.

CHAPTER X.

DEMOSTHENES CONTINUES HIS SPEECHES AGAINST PHILIP.

FROM the peace of 346 B.C. we may date a revolution in the Greek world. Philip had acquired a new position, and it was acknowledged that he had henceforth a right to take a part in Greek politics. Even Demosthenes had to recognise the fact of a change of sentiment towards him. Isocrates could argue more plausibly than ever that everything pointed to him as the true head and champion of Greece, and, consequently, as the predestined conqueror of Asia, the old antagonist of Greece.

The peace just concluded was soon seen to be a thoroughly hollow one. Philip, it was evident, had no intention of being really bound by it, any longer than it answered his purpose. This the Athenians could hardly fail to understand, however much they might try to deceive themselves; and their feeling towards him was made up of fear and anger. We might have thought that he could have at once organised a Greek confederacy against Persia with almost a certainty of success, but he seems to have been too cautious and astute to expose himself to any serious risks. His policy was to secure a yet firmer footing in the Greek world. Athens, he knew, was his only formidable enemy. There was still a possibility that she might rouse Greece against him, and overpower him by a coalition of which she would be the head. He must therefore endeavour to isolate her by political intrigues, and, by driving her out of the Chersonese, strike a fatal blow at the commerce on which her prosperity largely depended.

With these views he began to meddle with the politics of the Peloponnese. There circumstances favoured his designs. He had the opportunity of playing the part of champion and deliverer to the oppressed. Sparta was the great object of dread to the people of Argos, of Megalopolis, and of Messene. They could not imagine that they had any other enemy to fear. Thebes had hitherto been their protector, but Thebes was no longer in a condition to command their confidence. It was to Philip that they now not unnaturally looked. It was hardly to be expected that they would abstain from invoking his aid against a pressing and immediate danger, because it may have been suggested to them that they were thereby imperilling the best interests of Greece. What they wanted was help against Sparta, and this Philip promised them. He would, he said, soon be with them in person; and meanwhile he sent them some troops, and bade Sparta refrain from any attempt on Messene.

This was a clever movement on Philip's part, and Athens could not very well protest against it or seek to thwart it. All that could be said was that, judging from the past, it was an interference which ultimately meant mischief. Demosthenes succeeded in bringing the Athenians to this point of view. He induced them to send an embassy, himself being at the head of it, into the Peloponnese, the express object of which was to defeat Philip's diplomacy. He visited several of the cities, and addressed warnings to them based on the bad faith of Philip generally, and on his treatment of Olynthus particularly. He told them plainly that in their fear and hatred of Sparta they were allowing themselves to become his accomplices in enslaving and ruining Greece. It seems that one of the chief arguments on which he insisted was the utter impossibility of a sincere and hearty union between free states and a despot. This would be sure to impress the democratic party — always a powerful element in a Greek state. He was heard—so he tells us himself in one of his subsequent speeches—with approbation and applause, but he failed to convince. There were, as he says in another speech, those in every state who were willing to be controlled by a foreign power, if only they could get the upper hand of their fellow-citizens. The old love of freedom and of legal government, which had been the great glory of Greece, seemed to be on the wane. Still Demosthenes accomplished something. Philip thought it necessary to send envoys to Athens with some sort of apology for himself and his general policy; and an embassy also came, perhaps at his suggestion, from some of the states of the Peloponnese. Athens was in a perplexing position. Philip could plausibly say that the Athenians were unreasonably suspicious towards him, and even, in fact, disregarding the spirit of the peace recently concluded. The envoys from Argos and Messene might fairly complain of the seeming connection between Athens and Sparta, and argue that it was a menace to the liberties of the Peloponnese. It was a great and critical occasion, and called for able statesmanship. It was an opportunity to raise yet higher the character of Demosthenes as a public adviser, and he availed himself of it. In the speech which he delivered in B.C. 344, known as the second Philippic, he spoke out in the plainest language both against Philip's insinuations and against the ill-timed complaints of the Peloponnesian envoys. He vindicated at the same time his own policy, and denounced the Philippising faction, in which his rival Æschines was now a conspicuous figure.

Philip, he declares, was the great aggressor of the age; he was a plotter against the whole of Greece. He repeats what he had said as ambassador to the people of Messene by way of warning from the past :—

"Ye men of Messene, how do you think the Olynthians would have looked to hear anything against Philip at those times when he surrendered to them Anthemus, which all former kings of Macedonia claimed, when he cast out the Athenian colonists and gave them Potidæa, thereby incurring your enmity, and giving them the land to enjoy? Think you that they expected such treatment as they got, or would they have believed it if they had been told? Nevertheless, after enjoying for a brief space the possessions of others, they are for

a long period deprived by Philip of their own, shamefully expelled—not only vanquished, but betrayed by
one another and sold. In truth, these too close con-
nections with despots are not safe for free states.
There are manifold contrivances for the guarding and
defending of cities—as ramparts, walls, trenches, and
the like; these are all made with hands and demand
an outlay. But there is one common safeguard in the
nature of wise men which is a good security for all,
but especially for democracies against despots. What
do I mean? Mistrust. Keep this; hold to this; preserve this only, and you can never be injured. What
do ye desire? Freedom. Then do you not see that
with this Philip's very titles are at variance? Every
king and despot is a foe to freedom, an antagonist to
laws. Will ye not beware, lest in seeking to be delivered from war you find a master?"

Yet in a speech delivered three years afterwards,
which we shall shortly notice, Demosthenes suggests
that they might entertain the thought of seeking aid
even from Persia. The suggestion, perhaps, was only
made in desperation, and must not be taken as repre-
senting anything like a change of political sentiments.
To the last Demosthenes was a believer in free and
popular governments as opposed to tyrannies and des-
potisms. Still, as he has to admit, such governments
are liable to be out-manœuvred by cunning diplomacy.
So it had been with themselves, as he reminds them
in the present speech. They had been persuaded to
believe that Philip, if he became master of Thermo-

pylæ, would humble their old enemy Thebes, and give them Oropus and Eubœa in exchange for Amphipolis.

"All these declarations on the hustings," he says, with the Philippising party in his eye, "I am sure you remember, though you are not famous for remembering injuries. While the mischief is only coming and preparing, whilst we hear one another speak, I wish every man, though he know it well, to be reminded who it was persuaded you to abandon Phocis and Thermopylæ, by the possession of which Philip commands the road to Attica and Peloponnese, and has brought it to this, that you have now to deliberate, not about claims and interests abroad, but about the defence of your home and a war in Attica, which will be a grievous shock to every citizen when it comes; and indeed it commenced from that day of your infatuation. Had you not been then deceived, there would be nothing now to distress the State."

One point insisted on in this speech is, that the struggle in the Greek states was no longer, as it had hitherto been, one between aristocracy and democracy, but between Philip's party and its opponents.

The following year witnessed a memorable contest between Demosthenes and Æschines. It arose out of the embassies to Philip and the various negotiations with him, which ended, as we have seen, so unfortunately for Athens and Greece. Æschines, it will be remembered, was an adherent of the peace party of Eubulus; and Demosthenes now made a great effort

to discredit him, as being, in fact, corruptly responsible
for Philip's occupation of Thermopylæ, the destruction
of Phocis, and the new and powerful position which
he had been able to assume in Greece. The pleadings
of both the orators in this great cause have come down
to us, and they are specially valuable as supplying us
with materials for the history of an intricate period.
Demosthenes presses his attack with great vehemence,
and resorts, as he well knew how, to the most savage
invective. To our minds it is, as a work of art, one
of the least pleasing and satisfactory of his speeches.
There is a coarseness and vulgarity about the vitupera-
tion—and that, too, under circumstances in which very
strong condemnation of his rival must have been felt
to have been a mistake. He taunts Æschines with
having been all along the conscious tool of Philip's
cunning policy, when it was perfectly well known that
he had himself, from want of clear foresight perhaps,
not steadily opposed that policy at more than one critical point. He was not successful; but the victory won
by his rival was a very poor one. Æschines was ac-
quitted only by thirty votes. This implies that, on
the whole, public opinion was against him, though it
may have been felt that distinct and positive evidence
was wanting. We may infer that Demosthenes' political influence was very great. He failed probably because, as Dr Thirlwall remarks, he had an extremely
intricate case, and could not attack Æschines effectively without having from time to time to defend
himself and explain certain ambiguities in his own
share in the negotiations.

Athens, as has been said, was now particularly vulnerable in the Thracian Chersonese and the north of the Ægean. To these points the restless Philip directed his attention in 342-341 B.C. It could not be doubted that he was meditating the annexation of this important district, and the conquest of the Greek cities on the northern shores of the Propontis—Perinthus, Selymbria, and above all Byzantium. If he could achieve this, Athens would be completely paralysed. Her maritime supremacy would be at an end, and her supplies of corn would be cut off. She would cease to exist as a commercial power. Philip's designs on Athens in Thrace were not unlike those of Napoleon I. on England in his attacks on Egypt and Spain. It was argued in Parliament at the time, that in carrying on war with France in these countries, we were practically standing on our own defence. Demosthenes took the same line of argument against Philip. A force had been sent out from Athens to the Chersonese as an army of observation on Philip's movements. The general, Diopeithes, was an able, energetic man ; and it is interesting to us to know that he was the father of the poet Menander. There were some disputes between the Athenian colonists and the Cardians to the north of the Chersonese. Philip seemed disposed to favour the latter, upon which Diopeithes at once retaliated by invading Macedonian territory. He gained some successes, and for a while even deprived Philip of some of his recent conquests. Considering that the peace of 346 B.C. was still in force, Athens may be said to have been put in the wrong by her over-zealous general, and

Philip sent the people a despatch in which he formally complained of these encroachments. All his political adherents at Athens clamoured for the instant recall of Diopeithes. Like other Athenian generals, Diopeithes, who commanded some mercenaries, was almost compelled to provide for them by expeditions which could not be strictly justified. Still, it might be truly argued in his favour that he was really repelling a dangerous aggressor. And on this ground Demosthenes pleaded his cause, and argued that he should be continued in his command. The speech he delivered on this occasion —"On behalf of the Chersonese," as it has been entitled—contains the clear and powerful reasonings of a sagacious statesman.

The people, he maintains, ought to deal with their enemies before they call their own servants to account. It was very well for Philip to complain of an infringement of the peace in this particular instance ; but was it not notorious that he had himself deprived Athens of her own possessions ? It was a mere blind to say, as some said, that they must make up their minds to have either war or peace. "If it appears that from the very first Philip has robbed us of our territories, and has been all along incessantly gathering the spoil of other nations, Greek and barbarian, for the materials of an attack upon you, what do they mean by saying we must have war or peace ? "

"Consider what is actually going on. Philip is staying with a large army in Thrace, and sending for reinforcements, as eye-witnesses report, from Macedonia and Thessaly. Now, should he wait for the trade-winds, and then march to the siege of Byzantium, think ye that the Byzantines would persist in their present folly, and would not invite and implore your aid? I do not believe it. No; they will receive any people, even those they distrust more than us, sooner than surrender their city to Philip—unless, indeed, he is beforehand with them and captures it. If, then, we are unable to sail northward, and there be no help at hand, nothing can prevent their destruction. Well; let us say the Byzantines are infatuated and besotted. Very likely; yet they must be rescued, because it is good for Athens. Nor is it clear that he will not attack the Chersonese; nay, if we may judge from the 'etter he sent us, he says he will chastise the people in ⁄he Chersonese. If the present army be kept on foot, ıt will be able to defend that country, and attack some of Philip's dominions. But if it become disbanded, what shall we do if he march against the Chersonese? With such facts and arguments before you, so far from disbanding this army which Diopeithes is endeavouring to organise for Athens, you ought yourselves to provide an additional one, to support him with funds, and with other friendly co-operation."

In the following passage he inveighs against his political opponents, and the extreme licence of speech allowed to them in practically advocating the interests of Philip :—

"This, you must be convinced, is a struggle for existence. You cannot overcome your enemies abroad

till you have punished your enemies, his ministers, at
home. They will be the stumbling-blocks which prevent you reaching the others. Why, do you suppose,
Philip now insults you? To other people he at least
renders services though he deceives them, while he is
already threatening you. Look, for instance, at the
Thessalians. It was by many benefits conferred on
them that he seduced them into their present bondage.
And then the Olynthians, again,—how he cheated them,
first giving them Potidæa and several other places,
is really beyond description. Now he is enticing the
Thebans by giving up to them Bœotia, and delivering
them from a toilsome and vexatious war. Each of
these peoples did get a certain advantage; but some of
them have suffered what all the world knows; others
will suffer whatever may hereafter befall them. As
for you, I recount not all that has been taken from
you, but how shamefully have you been treated and
despoiled! Why is it that Philip deals so differently
with you and with others? Because yours is the only
state in Greece in which the privilege is allowed of
speaking for the enemy, and a citizen taking a bribe
may safely address the Assembly, though you have
been robbed of your dominions. It was not safe at
Olynthus to be Philip's advocate unless the Olynthian
commonalty had shared the advantage by possession
of Potidæa. It was not safe in Thessaly to be Philip's
advocate unless the people of Thessaly had secured the
advantage by Philip's expelling their tyrants and re-
storing the synod at Pylæ. It was not safe in Thebes,
until he gave up Bœotia to them and destroyed the

Phocians. Yet at Athens, though Philip has deprived you of Amphipolis and the territory round Cardia—nay, is making Euboea a fortress as a check upon us, and is advancing to attack Byzantium—it is safe to speak in Philip's behalf."

He thus concludes the speech :—

"I will sum up my advice and sit down. You must contribute money, and maintain the existing troops, rectifying any abuse you may discover, but not, on any accusation which somebody may bring, disbanding the force. Send out ambassadors everywhere to instruct, to warn, to accomplish what they can for Athens. Further, I say, punish your corrupt statesmen, execrate them at all times and places, and thereby prove that men of virtue and honourable conduct have consulted wisely both for others and for themselves."

It is satisfactory to learn that this speech was successful, and that Diopeithes, who certainly deserved well of his country, was continued in his command, and the Chersonese saved for Athens.

Demosthenes was now the leading Athenian statesman. He had shaken the influence of the peace party, and he seems to have still further strengthened his political position by a speech delivered about three months after that which we have just been considering. The speech in question has always been regarded as one of singular power. As far as we know, nothing new had occurred ; but Philip was still in Thrace, threatening the Chersonese and the northern shores of the

Propontis, and clearly had designs on Perinthus and Byzantium. Demosthenes repeats in substance the arguments he had recently urged. Greece, he says, is in the utmost peril from its miserable divisions and apathy, and from the unique position which it has allowed Philip to attain. As for Athens, " her affairs have been brought so low by carelessness and negligence, I fear it is a hard truth to say that if all the orators had sought to suggest, and you to pass, resolutions for the utter ruining of the commonwealth, we could not, methinks, be worse off than we are." It had been said at Athens in the speeches of some of the orators, " Wait till Philip declares war, and then it will be time to discuss how we shall resist him." Demosthenes' reply is,—

" If we wait till Philip avows that he is at war with us, we are the simplest of mortals; for he would not declare war, though he marched even against Athens and Piræus—at least, if we may judge from his conduct to others. When he sends his mercenaries into the Chersonese, which the king of Persia and all the Greeks acknowledge to be yours, what can be the meaning of such proceedings? He says he is not at war. But I cannot admit such conduct to be an observance of the peace. Far otherwise. I say that by his present advance into Thrace, by his intrigues in the Peloponnese, by the whole course of his operations with his army, he has been breaking the peace and making war upon you, —unless, indeed, you will say that those who establish military engines are not at war until they apply them to the walls. But that you will not say; for whoever prepares and contrives the means for my conquest, is at war with me before he hurls the dart or draws the bow. Should anything happen, what is the risk you run? The alienation of the Hellespont, the subjection of Megara and Eubœa to your enemy, the siding of the Peloponnese with him. Then, can I allow that one who sets such an engine at work against Athens is at peace with her? Quite the contrary. From the day that he destroyed Phocis I date his commencement of hostilities. So widely do I differ from your other advisers that I deem any discussion about the Chersonése or Byzantium out of place. Succour them —I advise that; watch that no harm befalls them; send all necessary supplies to your troops in that quarter: but let your deliberations be for the safety of all Greece, as being in the most extreme jeopardy."

The Greeks, he declares, must have utterly forgotten themselves in allowing a foreigner and a barbarian a licence in dealing with their affairs which they had never thought of according to such states as Athens or Sparta. This was monstrous, and implied a fatal degeneracy.

" I observe," says the orator, " that all people beginning from yourselves have conceded to Philip a right which in former days was the subject of contest in every Greek war. What is this? The right of doing what he pleases, openly fleecing and pillaging the Greeks one after another, attacking and enslaving their cities. You were at the head of the Greeks for seventy - three years, the Lacedæmonians for twenty-nine, and the Thebans had some power in these latter days after the battle of Leuctra. Yet neither you nor Lacedæmonians nor Thebans were ever licensed to act as you pleased. Far otherwise. When you, or rather the Athenians of that time, appeared to be dealing harshly with certain people, all the rest, even such as had no complaint against Athens, thought proper to side with the injured parties in a war against her. So, when the Lacedæmonians became masters and succeeded to your empire, on their attempting to encroach and make oppressive innovations, a general war was declared against them even by such as had no cause of complaint. But why mention other people? We ourselves and the Lacedæmonians, although at the outset we could not allege any mutual injuries, thought proper to make war for the injustice that we saw done to our neighbours. Yet all the faults committed by the Spartans in those thirty years, and by our ancestors in the seventy, are less than the wrongs which in thirteen incomplete years, while Philip has been uppermost, he has inflicted on the Greeks. Nay, they are scarcely a fraction of them, as I may easily and briefly show. Olynthus and Methone, and Apollonia and thirty-two cities on the borders of Thrace, I pass over —all which he has so cruelly destroyed that a visitor could scarcely tell if they were ever inhabited. And of Phocis, so considerable a people exterminated, I say nothing. But what is the condition of Thessaly? Has he not taken away her constitutions and her cities, and established tetrarchies, to parcel her out, not only by cities, but by provinces, for subjection? Are not the states of Eubœa now governed by despots, and Eubœa is an island near to Thebes and to Athens? Does he not expressly write in his epistles, "I am at peace with those who are willing to obey me"? Neither Greek nor barbaric land contains the man's ambition. And we, the Greek community, seeing and hearing this, instead of sending embassies to one another about it and expressing our indignation, are in such a miserable state, so entrenched in our separate towns, that to this day we can attempt nothing that interest or necessity requires; we cannot combine for succour and alliance; we look unconcernedly on the man's growing power, each resolving to enjoy the interval in which another is destroyed, not caring nor striving for the salvation of Greece. Whatever wrong the Greeks sustained from Lacedæmonians or from us, was at least inflicted by a genuine Greek people. It might be felt in the same manner as if a lawful son, born to a large fortune, committed some fault or error in the management of it. On that ground, one would consider him open to censure and to reproach; yet it could not be said he was an alien and not an heir to the property which he so dealt with. But if a slave or a spurious child wasted and spoilt that in which he had no interest, how much more heinous and hateful would all have pronounced it!"

On the decay of patriotism and the venality of public men throughout Greece, he speaks thus :—

"There must be some cause, some good reason, why
the Greeks were so eager for liberty then, and now are so
eager for servitude. There was something in the hearts
of the multitude then which there is not now, which
overcame the wealth of Persia, and maintained the freedom of Greece, and quailed not under any battle by sea
or land, the loss whereof has ruined all and thrown the
Greek world into confusion. What was this? No
subtlety or cleverness; simply this, that whoever took
a bribe from the aspirants to power or the corrupters of
Greece was universally abhorred. It was a fearful thing
to be convicted of bribery; the severest punishment was
inflicted on the guilty, and there was no intercession
or pardon. The favourable moments for enterprise
which fortune frequently offers to the careless against
the vigilant, to them that will do nothing against those
that discharge their entire duty, could not be bought
from orators or generals; no more could mutual con-
cord, nor distrust of tyrants and barbarians, nor anything of the kind. But now all such principles have
been sold as in open market, and principles imported
in exchange by which Greece is ruined and diseased.
What are they? Envy, when a man gets a bribe;
laughter, if he confesses it; mercy to the convicted;
hatred of those who denounce the crime,—all the usual
accompaniments of corruption. For as to ships and
men, and revenues and abundance of other material—
all, in fact, that may be reckoned as constituting national
strength, assuredly the Greeks of our day are more
fully and perfectly supplied with such advantages than
Greeks of the olden times. But they are all rendered

useless, unavailable, unprofitable by the agency of these traffickers."

This is indeed a powerful denunciation of a state of things which we know to be very possible, in which the corruption of public men is treated as a joke, and when exposed and detected, is hardly thought to deserve reprobation and punishment. If all that was best in Greece had really so utterly died out, it would seem that Demosthenes was wasting his breath in idle declamation. But we may well believe that he clung to the old Athenian ideal, and could not bring himself to despair of his country. And it is certain that this and the preceding speech produced an effect, and Athens made efforts which were temporarily successful. "The work of saving Greece," he told them before he sat down, "belongs to you; this privilege your ancestors bequeathed to you as the prize of many perilous exertions."

As one might expect, there were those who sought to persuade the Athenians that Philip's power for aggression had been greatly exaggerated, and that he was by no means so formidable as Sparta had once been, when she led the Peloponnesian confederacy. Demosthenes points out that Philip had introduced what was really a new method of warfare. Athens and Sparta, in the height of their power, had only been able to command a citizen militia from the states in league with them. Such a force was prepared only for a summer campaign, and could not always follow up its blows effectively. Philip, on the other hand, could take the field in winter as well as in summer. His troops were never disbanded, and they were under his sole direction. He was, in fact, to the Greeks what Napoleon was to the Austrians. An able and restless despot, at the head of a well-trained standing army, will often, for a time at least, have a decided advantage in war over a free and constitutional state.

The next year, 340 B.C., events occurred which completely justified the warnings of Demosthenes. Philip attempted the conquest of the cities on the Propontis, Perinthus and Byzantium. He was foiled by prompt intervention from Athens. There was for a brief space a doubt whether Byzantium would accept Athenian aid, so thoroughly had the city become estranged from Athens in consequence of the Social War. Demosthenes went thither at the head of an embassy, and the result was, that an alliance was concluded. Shortly afterwards, the conscientious and much - respected Phocion, though he differed politically from Demosthenes, sailed thither with a powerful armament and a force of Athenian citizens. Through the influence of Leon, one of the leading citizens of Byzantium, who had been Phocion's fellow-student at Athens in the Academy, they were admitted into the city, and charmed the Byzantines by their quiet and admirable behaviour. Succours also arrived from some of the islands of the Ægean—from Cos, Chios, Rhodes. Byzantium was now all but impregnable, and Philip was obliged to abandon the siege both of it and of Perinthus. Even his own territory was invaded by Phocion, and many of the Macedonian cruisers were captured. For Philip

it was a year of reverses, as for Athens it was one of
success and glory. The two cities on the Propontis
decreed her a vote of thanks, and displayed their
gratitude by erecting three colossal statues, represent-
ing Athens receiving a wreath at their hands in testimony of their deliverance. Demosthenes, too, had his
reward. No one could question that to his counsels
and energy they owed in great measure the preservation
of the Chersonese and their supremacy at sea. Corn
cheap and abundant was for the present assured to
them. The Athenian people were in a pleased and
grateful mood, and the Assembly passed a vote of
thanks to Demosthenes, which none of his many
political enemies dared to oppose.

CHAPTER XI.

CHÆRONEIA—FALL OF GREECE

WE must now hurry on to the decisive catastrophe which sealed the fate of Greece and of its political independence. Its glory had been to have been represented by an aggregate of free states, of which Athens was immeasurably the first in culture and civilisation. Its weakness and curse had been perpetual and all but irremediable rivalries and jealousies, which went far to neutralise its collective strength in the face of a real peril. It was now on the eve of a revolution which the Greek mind, in spite of many a warning from Demosthenes, had never been able to bring itself to contemplate as possible. He had done his best, as we have seen, to retard it amid endless discouragements, and to the last we shall find him faithful to the cause of which he never once seems to have allowed himself to despair. In the train of events which culminated in Chæroneia we find him bearing a conspicuous and honourable part.

Philip's career, as we have just seen, had been temporarily checked; and at the close of the year 340 B.C. Athens might almost congratulate herself on all danger having passed away. In the spring of 339 B.C. the King met with another disaster. He had plunged into the wilds of Scythia, north of the Danube, and had carried off a vast booty of flocks and herds from the barbarous people; but on his return through Thrace he was attacked by the Triballi, one of the fiercest and most warlike of the tribes of that dangerous region. We know what it is for a regular and well-equipped army to have to march through an intricate and hostile country. The king of Macedon, encumbered as he was with spoil, was taken at a disadvantage, and if not actually defeated, he was at least worsted, lost his plunder, and was himself badly wounded. Thus the year 339 B.C. seemed one of good omen for Athens and for Greece. And thanks to the vigorous efforts of Demosthenes in the way of naval reform, the Athenian fleet was now supreme in the Ægean.

Meanwhile a new sacred war in behalf of the god and temple of Delphi was unfortunately breaking out. It arose out of incidents which may seem to us comparatively trifling. An Amphictyonic Council had assembled at Delphi in the autumn of 340 B.C., and Athens was represented by Æschines. The fruitful plain of Crisa, stretching inland from the Gulf of Corinth to the town of Amphissa, under the mountains of Parnassus, was the consecrated possession of the Delphic god. It was holy ground, and to till or to plant it had been forbidden with a tremendous curse. Part of it, however, adjacent to the town and port of Cirrha, had, almost with the sanction of Greek opinion, been occupied and brought into cultivation for a long period by the Locrians. Between them and the Phocians there had been a long-standing feud, which reached a climax in the recent Sacred War. The Locrians in that war had sided with Philip and the Thebans against their sacrilegious neighbours. Consequently, after the destruction of Phocis, they had a sore feeling towards Athens as the ally of the Phocians. One of their deputies, on the occasion of which we are speaking, rudely gave expression to this feeling, and went so far as to revile the Athenians, and to imply that an alliance with such a people was in itself equivalent to the guilt of sacrilege. Possibly the man may have wished to curry favour with the Thebans, to whose disgust some golden shields had just been set up by the Athenians in a new chapel at Delphi, with an inscription commemorating the victory of Athens over Persia and Thebes at Platæa a century and a half ago. This small incident was dwelt upon by the Locrian orator in violent and intemperate language. " Do not," said he, " permit the name of the Athenian people to be pronounced among you at this holy season. Turn them out of the sacred ground like men under a curse."

Æschines, the Athenian representative (he describes the affair himself in his great speech against Ctesiphon, or, we may say, against Demosthenes), savagely retorted. He pointed to the plain of Crisa, visible from the spot where they were assembled. " You see," he said, " that plain cultivated by the Locrians of Amphissa, covered with their farm-buildings. You have under your eyes the port of Cirrha, consecrated by your forefathers' oath, now occupied and fortified."

Then he caused the ancient oracle, the oath with its dreadful curse, to be read out before the Council. "Here am I," he went on to say, "ready to defend the property of the god according to your forefathers' oath. I stand prepared to clear my own city of her obligations. Do you take counsel for yourselves. You are here to pray for blessings to the gods, publicly and individually. Where will you find voice or heart or courage to offer such a prayer if you let these accursed Locrians of Amphissa remain unpunished?"

The appeal of Æschines produced an instantaneous effect. The excitement was prodigious; and the Council in a moment of fury passed a resolution that on the morrow all the population of Delphi were to assemble with spades and pickaxes, and sweep away from the sacred plain every trace of the impious tillage and cultivation. Next day this mad proposal was actually carried into effect. The furious mob rushed across the plain into the town of Cirrha, and pillaged and fired the place. On their return, however, they were met by the Locrians of Amphissa with an armed force, and obliged to take refuge in Delphi. There was no bloodshed, even under these circumstances of provocation, as the aggrieved owners of the destroyed property were restrained by a sentiment of reverence for the Amphictyonic Council. Here is, indeed, a striking evidence of the respect felt for the traditions of the god of Delphi and his ancient temple, the centre of the religious life of Greece. Again, on the following day, the Council met, and after warm praise had been bestowed on Athens as the avenger of Apollo's rights, the people of Amphissa were denounced as having incurred the guilt of sacrilege; and it was finally decided that the Amphictyonic deputies should shortly assemble at Thermopylæ to consider how they were to be punished.

A new sacred war was thus in effect begun six years after the disastrous termination of the previous war in 346 B.C. That had ended in the destruction of a member of the Greek community; this was to end in the ruin and fall of Greece. The danger was not at once perceived at Athens. We cannot wonder at this. Æschines' vindication of his countrymen at the Council might well seem spirited and patriotic. Athens, through him, had stood forward as the champion of the god of Delphi. It was easy for him to argue that those who took a different view, and regretted the rash act to which the Amphictyons had been prompted by his oratory, were little better than the paid agents of those sacrilegious Locrians, who had allowed one of their speakers openly to insult Athens. Demosthenes, however—so he tells us—at once declared in the Assembly, " You are bringing war into Attica, Æschines— an Amphictyonic war." The popular sentiment at the time was in favour of Æschines, and this his political rival must have known and felt. Still, Demosthenes was able—a proof this of the high respect in which he was held—to persuade the people not to send any deputies to the special congress at Thermopylæ, which was to deliberate on the punishment of the Locrians. Thebes, too, allowed herself to be unrepresented. War was decided on; the Locrian territory was invaded, and a fine imposed on the Locrians, the payment of which, however, the army was not sufficiently powerful to compel.

The congress of which we have just spoken was not the regular Amphictyonic meeting. This was held in the autumn of 339 B.C. Philip by that time had returned to his kingdom. The meeting was now at Delphi; and Athens, as might be expected, took part in it. Æschines again was one of her representatives. It was on this occasion that the fatal step was taken of invoking the aid of Philip. It is not very difficult to understand how such a vote was carried. Macedon itself was a member of the Council; and so, too, were several states like Thessaly and Phthiotis, which now were simply Macedonian dependencies. Æschines, it may be from really corrupt motives, supported the vote. Accordingly Philip was elected general of the Amphictyonic army; and a request was forwarded to him that " he would march to the aid of Apollo and the Amphictyons, and not suffer the rights of the god to be invaded by the impious Locrians of Amphissa."

The die was now cast. The peril to Greece might possibly even yet have been warded off; but it was great and imminent. And Thebes and Athens, on whom all now depended, were still notoriously unreconciled. Philip, of course, instantly accepted the Council's invitation. He would enter Greece as the representative of a holy cause, as well as the head of a very powerful army. From Thermopylæ he marched straight through Phocis to Elateia, the chief Phocian town and the key to southern Greece. It was not sixty miles from the Athenian frontier. Here he halted and began to establish a regular camp. This was in itself alarming. His next step was to send a message to Thebes inviting the co-operation of the Thebans in an attack on Attica.

In a graphic passage in the most famous of his speeches, Demosthenes describes the impression made at Athens by the news that Philip was at Elateia.

"It was evening," he says, "when a messenger arrived with tidings for the Presidents that Elateia was taken. They rose instantly from the public supper-table; some drove the people from the stalls in the Forum, and set fire to the wicker-work in order to clear the space; others sent for the generals, and called the trumpeter. The whole city was in commotion. Next morning, at break of day, the Presidents convoked the Senate in the Senate House, and you repaired to the Assembly, and before the Senate could enter upon business, or draw up the decree to be submitted to you, all the people had taken their seats in the Pnyx. When the Senate had entered—when the Presidents had communicated the intelligence which had been brought to them—when the messenger had been introduced, and related his tidings,—the herald made proclamation, 'Who desires to speak?' But no one came forward. Again and again did the herald repeat the proclamation; our country's voice called out for a man to speak and save her; for the voice of the herald raised at the law's command should be regarded as the voice of our common country. Still not a man came forward."

In this crisis Demosthenes gave his counsel. It was to the following effect:—

"I said," he tells us, "that the dismay of those who suppose that Philip could still count on the Thebans must proceed from an ignorance of the real state of the case. If that were so, it would not be at Elateia — it would be on our own frontier — that we should hear of Philip. That he had come to make things ready for him in Thebes I knew well. But mark, I said, how the matter stands. Every man in Thebes whom money can buy, every man whom flattery can gain, has long ago been secured. But he is totally unable to prevail upon those who have withstood him from the beginning, and who are opposing him still. What, then, has brought Philip to Elateia? He hopes, by a military demonstration in your neighbourhood, and by bringing up his army, to raise the courage and confidence of his friends, and to strike terror into his enemies, so that they may be frightened or coerced into surrendering what hitherto they have been unwilling to concede. If, then, I said, we choose at this crisis to remember every ill turn which the Thebans have done us, and to distrust them and treat them as enemies, in the first place we shall be doing the very thing which Philip most desires; and next, I fear that, his present adversaries embracing his cause, they will all fall on Attica together. If you will be advised by me, and regard what I am about to say as matter for reflection rather than for disputation, I believe that my counsel will obtain your approbation, and be the means of averting the peril which now threatens the State. What, then, do I advise? First, shake off this panic—or rather change the direction of your fears from yourselves to the Thebans, for they are far nearer ruin than ourselves. The danger is theirs before it is ours. Next, let all citizens of military age and all your cavalry march to Eleusis, and show yourselves to the world in arms, that the Thebans who are on your side may be as bold as their adversaries, and speak out in the cause of right, with the assurance that, if there is at Elateia a force at hand to support the party who have sold their country to Philip, your forces are no less at the disposal of those who would fight for freedom, and ready to succour them in case of attack. Make no conditions with the Thebans. It would be unworthy on such an occasion. Simply declare your readiness to succour them, on the assumption that their peril is imminent, and that you are in a better position than they to forecast the future. If they accept our offer and adopt our views, we shall have attained our object, and pursued a policy worthy of our country. If anything should mar the project, they will have only themselves to blame, and we shall have nothing to blush for in our part of the transaction."

Such was the counsel of Demosthenes in this great crisis. It was instantly adopted by the Assembly without a dissentient voice. The matter did not stop here. "Not only did I make a speech," Demosthenes tells us, "but I proposed a decree. Not only did I propose the decree, but I went upon the embassy. Not only went I on the embassy, but I prevailed on the Thebans." At Thebes the orator had to confront the envoys of Philip, backed up by the Philippising party and by the old Theban animosity towards Athens. Each embassy was heard, according to Greek custom, before the Theban Assembly. Philip had eloquent advocates who suggested plausible reasons why he should be allowed to march through Bœotia and to humble the old enemy of Thebes. Unfortunately, we have not the reply of Demosthenes. We know, how-ever, from the historian of the time, Theopompus, that he rose to the occasion, and convinced the wavering Thebans, by an impressive appeal to every Greek and patriotic sentiment, that it was their duty and interest to accept the offered alliance. It was a signal triumph —one, too, achieved under extreme difficulties.

It must, indeed, have been a proud moment for De-mosthenes when he saw his country's army march across the Attic frontier and enter Bœotia at the Theban invitation. All distrust and jealousy had now passed away; and the two states, between whom there had been long and bitter rivalry, had at last made up their mind to co-operate in a common cause. As it had been at Byzantium, so was it now at Thebes. The Athenian soldiers received a hearty welcome, and were hospitably entertained in the houses of the city.

" With such cordiality," says Demosthenes in his speech on the Crown, "did they welcome you, that while their own infantry and cavalry were quartered outside the walls, they received your army within their city and

their homes, among their wives and all that they held
most precious.   On that day the Thebans gave you, in
the face of all mankind, three of the highest testimonials
—the first of your valour, the second of your justice,
and the third of your good conduct.   For in choosing
to fight with you rather than against you, they judged
that you were better soldiers, and engaged in a better
cause than Philip; and by intrusting to you that
which they in common with all mankind regard with
the most jealous watchfulness, their children and their
wives, they manifested their confidence in your good
conduct.   The result showed that they were well war-
ranted in their trust; for after the army entered their
city, not a single complaint, well or ill founded, was
made against you, so orderly was your behaviour.   And
when your soldiers stood side by side with their hosts
in two successive engagements, their discipline, their
equipments, their courage, were such as not only to
challenge criticism, but to command admiration."

Two slight successes, indeed, were won by the united
armies of Thebes and Athens.   Of the campaign we
have no detailed narrative, and of the final battle we
have but an imperfect and unsatisfactory description.
It would have been most interesting to have had such
an account of it as Xenophon has given us of Leuctra
and Mantineia.   It was fought near Chæroneia, close
to the borders of Phocis,—a town of little importance,
but memorable from its historical associations.   More
than two centuries afterwards, a great victory was won
there by Sulla over an army of Mithridates.   It was,

too, the birthplace of Plutarch, and to it he retired
from Rome in his old age. On this occasion it would
seem that as to numbers the forces were evenly
matched. But the Greek army was without a general
of any marked ability. Phocion, by far the best
Athenian officer, was absent with the fleet in the
Ægean. A commander of the first order—a man, for
example, of the calibre of Epameinondas—might have
turned the scale, and no doubt would have done so
had there been a powerful contingent from Sparta and
the Peloponnese. United Greece, it is probable, could
even yet have crushed Philip. As it was, all may be
said to have depended on Athens and Thebes, though
a few other states furnished some soldiers. The Macedonian army was both skilfully commanded and was
very formidable in itself. It was led by Philip and
by his young son Alexander; and he it was, it appears,
to whom the victory was mainly due. He was opposed
to the Theban phalanx—the Sacred band, as it was called
—which fell fighting to a man. It is certain that the
battle was obstinately contested, and almost equally
certain that it was decided by superiority of general-
ship. The Athenians, after their wont, dashed upon
the enemy with furious impetuosity; but a citizen
militia, however brave and enthusiastic, unless they
were victorious at the first onset, could hardly be
expected to stand long against such troops as
Philip's trained veterans. They did, according to one
account, put the enemy to flight, and their general
exclaimed, "Let us pursue them even to Macedonia."
But the end was complete defeat for the Greek army,

and the year 338 B.C. witnessed the fall of Greek independence.

To Thebes the result was immediate ruin. Its citadel was at once occupied by a Macedonian garrison, and its government put under Macedonian control. Athens, 1000 of whose citizens had fallen, and 2000 been taken prisoners, was in an agony of distress; but she did not allow herself to despair. Isocrates, still alive in his 99th year, though he had been politically opposed to Demosthenes and had cherished the idea of a united Greece under the leadership of the king of Macedon, was heart-broken, and refused to live any longer. He was a true patriot; and

" That dishonest victory
At Chæroneia, fatal to liberty,
Killed with report that old man eloquent."

Demosthenes had fought in his countrymen's ranks, and had fled with the rest; but though his enemies taunted him with cowardice, he had the honour of pronouncing the funeral panegyric over the fallen. His counsels had been followed; the result had been disastrous; yet he still evidently retained the confidence and esteem of the people. Athens recovered her captured citizens without ransom, for the conqueror chose to be generous; but the cause for which she had fought was a thing of the past. Demosthenes must have felt after Chæroneia as Pitt felt after Austerlitz when he closed the map of Europe. His efforts had been rewarded with the gratitude of his countrymen, but they had not been rewarded with success.

CHAPTER XII.

CONTEST BETWEEN DEMOSTHENES AND ÆSCHINES.

PHILIP was now the acknowledged head of the Greek
world. Phocion, Athens' best soldier, as well as a highly
honourable citizen, told the Athenians that they must
acquiesce in this result. Demosthenes had not a word
left to say on foreign policy. The subject was, in fact,
closed. He was continually and virulently attacked
by his political opponents, but he was too strong for
them. He spoke the funeral eulogy at the obsequies
of the slain in the great battle—an honour to which he
was chosen in preference to Æschines, as well as to
Demades, who had negotiated the peace. He held,
too, more than one important office. He was treasurer
of the Theoric fund, which provided Athens with her
grand dramatic entertainments; and in this capacity he
had a considerable control over the finances generally.
He was also superintendent of the city walls and fortifications. He must thus have had the character of an
able and upright man of business. And he continued
to follow the profession of the bar, and found abundant
employment.

In 336 B.C. Philip was assassinated. It seems that

Demosthenes, though at the time he was mourning the death of an only daughter, showed an excessive joy by appearing in public in a white dress with a garland on his head, and performing a solemn sacrifice of thanksgiving. Could he have indulged in the dream that all was now to be reversed, and that Greece was again to be free? Macedon, no doubt, with its sudden growth of power, might have collapsed, had Philip's son and successor been an imbecile. And it appears that Demosthenes thought meanly of the young Alexander. He compared him to Margites, the hero of a comic poem which tradition attributed to Homer. Margites was a man who "knew many things, but knew them all badly;" he was a sort of "Jack of all trades and master of none." Alexander was famous for the variety of his studies and pursuits; and it was this, it may be supposed, which gave point to the comparison. Demosthenes' idea of him was, that he was a studious, bookish young man, of whom the world would never hear much. The fact that he was only twenty years of age at the time of his father's death may have reasonably encouraged Demosthenes to believe that Greece had some chance of throwing off the yoke imposed on her by her defeat at Chæroneia. He did not think it wrong to correspond with Persia, and to avail himself of Persian gold, with the view of frustrating Philip's designs on Asia. We can hardly censure him for this, when we remember that it was done for the patriotic purpose of freeing Greece from its present position of a Macedonian dependency. If he used questionable means, he at least had the merit of standing by the old cause. But, of course, it was easy for his enemies to represent his conduct in an odious light.

Three years after Chæroneia, Alexander, after a successful expedition into Thrace, and a victory over the barbarous and warlike Getæ on the further bank of the Danube, hurried with marvellous rapidity southwards to crush a movement of revolt in Thebes. There was, as we have seen, a Macedonian garrison in the city. There was, too, a powerful political party which urged prompt submission. Alexander himself was particularly anxious not to drive matters to extremities. But the party which had instigated the movement knew that they could not hope for mercy ; and, by appealing to the cause of Greek freedom, persuaded the people to reject all offers of peace. The unhappy city was captured by assault, and every house but that of the poet Pindar and those of his descendants was razed to the ground.

> " The great Emathian conqueror bade spare
> The house of Pindarus, when temple and tower
> Went to the ground."

It was a terrible doom, but it was approved by the towns of Bœotia ; and but for the brief grandeur to which Thebes rose under Epameinondas, and her share in the battle of Chæroneia, we may almost say it was deserved. She had been a traitor to the common cause in the great struggle with Persia ; and afterwards, with a peculiar baseness, she had urged Sparta to slaughter, in cold blood, the brave Platæans, whose only crime was, that they had sided with Athens in the Pelopon-

nesian War. Thebes was now blotted out of existence.
Again Athens trembled. Alexander, there was reason
to believe, was magnanimous; but it was impossible to
say how he might deal with a city which had been so
persistently hostile to his father. At the suggestion of
Demades, an embassy of congratulation was sent to
him. The people were to express their joy not only on
his safe return from the Danube, but on the extinction
of Thebes. It was, as Dr Thirlwall happily calls it,
"impudent obsequiousness." Alexander's answer was
a demand for the surrender of the nine chief anti-
Macedonian orators,—Demosthenes, of course, included.
But the demand was waived, chiefly, it seems, through
the opportune intervention of Phocion, whom Alexander highly respected.

The next year he crossed the Hellespont into Asia.
Four years from that time sufficed for the overthrow
of the Persian empire. Darius, the last king of Persia,
was murdered in 330 B.C. That same year witnessed
an abortive attempt in Greece against Macedonian
supremacy. It was bravely led by a king of Sparta,
who fell in a hard-fought battle near Megalopolis with
Antipater, to whom Alexander had intrusted his kingdom during his absence. Greece could now no longer
even dream of independence. Anything like an anti-
Macedonian policy would be preposterous; and there
was thus an opportunity at Athens of attempting to
rouse popular feeling against any statesman who had
advocated that policy, the end of which had been so
fatal to Greece.

It was under these circumstances that Æschines

made a great effort to crush his old rival. It had been proposed by Ctesiphon, in the year after Chæroneia, that a public testimonial to the worth of Demosthenes should be given him in the form of a golden crown; and that the honour should be proclaimed on the occasion of one of those great dramatic festivals, when the city was crowded with visitors from every part of Greece. The proposal had been approved by the Athenian Senate, but it had yet to be submitted to the popular assembly. Æschines at the time denounced it as unconstitutional, and opposed it by one of the recognised modes of legal procedure. Technically, indeed, the motion of Ctesiphon was illegal. Demosthenes, as we have stated, was holding two offices; he was superintendent of fortifications and treasurer of the Theoric fund. It was contrary to Athenian law to bestow the honour of a crown on an officer before his accounts had been audited; it was also forbidden that such an honour should be proclaimed anywhere else than in the Pnyx, the regular place of the people's assembly. According to the motion of the proposer, it would have been proclaimed in the theatre. Æschines could, therefore, argue that it was in two points illegal. But he wished to win a decisive victory; and he accordingly waited for some years, and finally rested his case on the argument that Demosthenes, as a public man, was undeserving of the honour. It is this which gives interest to his extant speech. He laboured to convince the Athenians that his rival could not have been thoroughly sincere in his anti-Macedonian professions, because he had let slip three important opportunities. Demosthenes had done nothing, so he argued, when Alexander first crossed into Asia; or when he was supposed to be in great jeopardy just before the battle of Issus in 333 B.C.; or lastly, when Sparta, as has been stated, made an attempt at resistance. It was in the year of this unsuccessful attempt—the year 330 B.C., when Macedon was triumphant both in Asia and Greece—that this memorable cause between the two rival orators was heard before the Athenian assembly. As might have been expected, there was a numerous gathering both of citizens and strangers, very many of whom were well qualified to be keen critics of the great contest.

The question really to be decided—and this was the issue which Æschines was anxious to raise—was, Had Demosthenes been a good or bad citizen? had he honestly at all times and seasons stood by the cause in which he so earnestly professed to believe? Demosthenes' reply to this question is the vindication of his political life. The cause for which he had exerted himself, though finally unsuccessful, was, he maintains, the true and the right cause. Had he foreseen the end from the beginning, he would have spoken and acted as he did. He reviews his policy from the peace of 346 B.C., concluded just after Philip's destruction of Phocis, down to the king's death ten years afterwards. To all this he looks back with satisfaction and pride. In defending himself he attacks his rival, and denounces him as really the author of the calamities which had fallen on the Greek world. It was through the diplomacy of Æschines, he declares, that

Philip was admitted to Thermopylæ, the beginning of all the subsequent mischief. If it was dreadful to think of Greece being under a foreign master, it was a glorious fact that Athens had done her best to avert such a disgrace.

This is the drift and purport of the great speech on the Crown, as it is usually called. It has been well described by Mr Grote as " a funeral oration on extinct Athenian and Grecian freedom." " It breathes," says Dr Thirlwall, " the spirit of that high philosophy which, whether learnt in the schools or from life, has consoled the noblest of our kind in prisons and on scaffolds, and under every persecution of adverse fortune, but in the tone necessary to impress a mixed multitude with a like feeling, and to elevate it for a while into a sphere above its own."

Some passages from this oration have already been quoted in the preceding chapter; and it is due to the reader to give him some further specimens of, perhaps, the greatest of all the oratorical efforts of Demosthenes.

Here is a passage in which the speaker dwells on the generous and magnanimous temper of his countrymen in their best days :—

" Let me for a moment bring before your eyes one or two of the brightest passages in the history of our times. Lacedæmon was paramount by sea and land ; she had a belt of garrisons about the frontiers of our territory; Eubœa, Tanagra, all Bœotia, Megara, Ægina, Cleonæ, every island on the coast. We had neither ships nor walls; we were in no want (had we chosen to remember the Decelean war) of grievances either against Corinth or Thebes. And yet the arms of Athens were seen at Haliartus, and in a few days after at Corinth. You had something better to do than to recall the injuries of the past. . . .

"The sacrifice in either case was not made for a benefactor, neither was it made without risk. You held that no reason for abandoning to their fate men who had thrown themselves on your compassion. Honour and renown were a sufficient motive to lead you into danger, and who shall say you were wrong? Life must cease; death must come at some time, though one should steal into a cellar to avoid him. The brave are ever ready to set forth on the path of glory, armed with high hope and courage, prepared to accept without a murmur the fate which heaven may ordain. Thus did your forefathers; thus did the elders among yourselves, who interposed and frustrated the attempts of the Thebans after their victory at Leuctra to destroy Sparta, though from Sparta you had experienced neither friendship nor good offices, but many grievous wrongs. You neither quailed before the power and renown which Thebes then possessed, nor were you deterred by any thought of your past treatment by Sparta. Thus did you proclaim to all the Greeks, that how much soever any of them may offend against you, you reserve your resentment for other occasions; but that if danger threaten their existence or their liberties, you will take no account of—you will not even remember—your wrongs."

This is his answer to those who persisted in saying that it was Philip—Philip alone—who had brought all their troubles on them :—

" Do not go about repeating that Greece owes all her misfortunes to one man. No, not to one man, but to many abandoned men distributed throughout the different states, of whom, by earth and heaven, Æschines is one. If the truth were to be spoken without reserve, I should not hesitate to call him the common scourge of all the men, the districts, and the cities which have perished ; for the sower of the seed is answerable for the crop. I am astonished you did not turn your faces from him the moment you beheld him ; but thick darkness would seem to veil your eyes."

He maintains that the action of the State had been right and honourable, though it had failed.

" I affirm that if the future had been apparent to us all—if you, Æschines, had foretold it and proclaimed it at the top of your voice instead of preserving total silence,—nevertheless the State ought not to have deviated from her course, if she had regard to her own honour, the traditions of the past, or the judgment of posterity. As it is, she is looked upon as having failed in her policy,—the common lot of all mankind when such is the will of heaven ; but if, claiming to be the foremost state of Greece, she had deserted her post, she would have incurred the reproach of betraying Greece to Philip. If we had abandoned without a struggle all which our forefathers braved every danger to win, who would not have spurned you, Æschines ? God forbid that I should so speak of the State as of myself. How could we have looked in the face the strangers who flock to our city, if things had reached their present pass— Philip the chosen leader and lord of all—while others without -our assistance had borne the struggle to avert this consummation? We! who have never in times past preferred inglorious safety to peril in the path of honour. Is there a Greek or a barbarian who does not know that Thebes at the height of her power, and Sparta before her — ay, and even the king of Persia himself—would have been only glad to compromise with us, and that we might have had what we chose, and possessed our own in peace, had we been willing to obey orders and to suffer another to put himself at the head of Greece? But it was not possible,—it was not a thing which the Athenians of those days could do. It was against their nature, their genius, and their traditions; and no human persuasion could induce them to side with a wrong-doer because he was powerful, and to embrace subjection because it was safe. No; to the last our country has fought and jeopardised herself for honour and glory and pre-eminence. A noble choice, in harmony with your national character, as you testify by your respect for the memories of your ancestors who have so acted. And you are in the right; for who can withhold admiration from the heroism of the men who shrank not from leaving their city and their fatherland, and embarking in their war-ships, rather than submit to foreign dictation? Why, Themistocles, who counselled this step, was elected general; and the man who counselled submission was stoned to death — and not he

only, for his wife was stoned by your wives, as he was
by you. The Athenians of those days went not in
quest of an orator or a general who could help them to
prosperous slavery; but they scorned life itself, if it
were not the life of freedom. Each of them regarded
himself as the child not only of his father and of his
mother, but of his country; and what is the difference?
He who looks on himself as merely the child of his
parents, awaits death in the ordinary course of nature;
while he who looks on himself as the child also of his
country, will be ready to lay down his life rather than
see her enslaved, and will hold death itself less terrible
than the insults and indignities which the citizens of a
state in slavery to the foreigner must endure. . . .

" Do I take credit to myself for having inspired you
with sentiments worthy of your ancestors? Such presumption would expose me to the just rebuke of every
man who hears me. What I maintain is, that these
very sentiments are your own; that the spirit of
Athens was the same before my time,—though I do
claim to have had a share in the application of these
principles to each successive crisis. Æschines, therefore, when he impeaches our whole policy, and seeks
to exasperate you against me as the author of all your
alarms and perils, in his anxiety to deprive me of
present credit, is really labouring to rob you of your
everlasting renown. If by your vote against Ctesiphon
you condemn my policy, you will pronounce yourselves
to have been in the wrong, instead of having suffered
what has befallen you through the cruel injustice of
fortune. But it cannot be: you have not been in the

wrong, men of Athens, in doing battle for the freedom and salvation of all; I swear it by your forefathers, who bore the battle's brunt at Marathon; by those who stood in arms at Platæa; by those who fought the sea-fight at Salamis; by the heroes of Artemisium, and many more whose resting-place in our national monuments attests that, as our country buried, so she honoured, all alike — victors and vanquished. She was right; for what brave men could do, all did, though a higher power was master of their fate."

This, perhaps, is the most striking of the many striking passages in this great speech. Demosthenes carried his audience with him. His rival did not obtain a fifth of the votes. His position as an orator and statesman was destroyed. His discomfiture had been witnessed by the whole Greek world. In his mortification he left his native city for Rhodes, where he set up a school of rhetoric. The story was told that he once declaimed to his pupils the speech which had driven him into exile; and in reply to the applause with which it was greeted, exclaimed, "What if you had heard the beast himself speak-it?"

CHAPTER XIII.

LAST DAYS OF DEMOSTHENES.

DEMOSTHENES had won a splendid triumph, which he survived eight years. But they were years by no means unclouded. They were darkened by an unfortunate incident, which we proceed briefly to narrate.

From 330 to 324 B.C., we hear nothing of the great orator. Athens, in fact, had no politics for him to discuss. He could have had nothing to do but to advise private clients. By the year 324 Alexander had returned from that long expedition in which he had carried his army through the heart of Asia to the banks of the Indus. He had left behind him one of his old Macedonian friends in the government of the rich satrapy of Babylonia. Harpalus (this was the man's name) was greedy and extravagant, and wasted the resources of his province in a luxury which he had learnt during his residence in the East. It was said that he loaded his table with the most costly delicacies, and filled his gardens with exotic plants of every variety. He had found it convenient to please the people of Athens by splendid presents, and particularly by very liberal gifts of wheat for free and general distribution. For all this he had received votes of thanks and been made an Athenian citizen. He was afraid, however, to face Alexander, who, he well knew, showed no mercy to delinquent satraps. So he fled from Asia to Europe with an immense treasure of 5000 talents (about a million and a quarter pounds sterling), and landed at Cape Sunium, in Attica. He might reasonably flatter himself that he would not be an unwelcome visitor at Athens, but in this he was disappointed. There was the fear of the wrath of Alexander; and the fear, too, that Harpalus might possibly intend to assume the position of a tyrant or despot. His offers, whatever they were, were rejected; but there was a debate in the Assembly, and a rumour reached Alexander that Athens had received him and his armament. This was at the time untrue; but when he sent away his ships and asked leave to be admitted into the city with a few personal attendants, the people, remembering his past favours, no longer refused. Having gained his point, he tried to persuade them that they might defy Alexander with a prospect of success, and that he was himself able and willing to furnish them with the necessary funds. Some of the orators supported his views. But he could do nothing with Phocion or with Demosthenes. This was fatal to his project. Soon there came envoys from Antipater, Alexander's deputy in Macedonia, requiring his surrender. But this both Phocion and Demosthenes, notwithstanding the danger of the crisis, opposed. So alarmed, however, were the people at the thought of Alexander's probable vengeance, that they decided on arresting Harpalus and sequestrating his treasure till they could learn what view Alexander took of the matter; and this much they did on the motion of Demosthenes himself. It seems possible, as has been suggested, that Demosthenes proposed this motion with an *arrière-pensée*, and may have wished to detain Harpalus and his treasure, and to wait the course of events. Harpalus contrived to escape; but his treasure—that part of it at least which he had brought to Athens after dismissing his fleet, and which amounted, according to statements made by Demosthenes on his authority, to about 720 talents—remained behind. This, of course, ought to have been returned— and the people were, it seems, prepared to do so; but when the money was counted it was found that there was no more than 350 talents, barely half the original sum. How was the deficiency to be explained? There was a great stir and outcry. People said that it must have been used in bribery, and that the missing money must have stuck to the fingers of the orators and public men. There was a general feeling that somebody ought to be punished, but there was not a scrap of evidence against any one, and no means of procuring it.

Demosthenes proposed to have the affair investigated by the court of Areopagus. It was not easy to see what better course could have been taken. At the same time, the members of that court must have felt that they could hardly hope, under the circumstances, to arrive at a perfectly satisfactory result. No doubt they commanded the public confidence, as they were all men of age and experience, and were from their position above the motives which occasionally swayed other courts. Great latitude was allowed them; and practically they often decided cases not simply on the evidence before them, but on hearsay, and on that personal knowledge which men in their rank would be sure to possess. They took the utmost pains with the present inquiry, and were engaged on it for six months. They went so far as to search the houses of the principal public men, with the exception of one who had been lately married—an exception perhaps to be attributed to a sense of delicacy. At last they published their report, with a list of the names of persons whom they considered chargeable with having improperly possessed themselves of the missing money.

In this list appeared the name of Demosthenes as a debtor to the amount of twenty talents. The next step was to give the accused parties the choice of taking their trial or of paying the sum with which the Areopagus had debited them. Of those brought to trial, Demosthenes was the first. He was tried before a jury of 1500 of his fellow-citizens, was found guilty, and sentenced to pay a fine of fifty talents (about £12,000). It is very possible that among the jury which condemned him there may have been many who wished to please Alexander, and many, too, of the friends of Harpalus. It must, however, be remembered that the decision of the Areopagus could not fail to influence their verdict. Demosthenes would not or could not pay the fine. He was imprisoned, but in a few days was able to escape to Trœzen, in the territory of Argos. It was but a few months that he remained there.

We can hardly bring ourselves to believe that he was really guilty. Of course we can judge only by probabilities; and it is certain that the court of Areopagus must have had grounds for their suspicion. We must bear in mind that they merely drew up a list of persons whose case in their opinion required further judicial inquiry. There is no reason for assuming that they regarded the guilt of Demosthenes as certain. The inquiry was long and difficult; and the decision ultimately arrived at could have been hardly meant to express confident assurance. If Demosthenes publicly stated, on Harpalus's authority, the amount of the treasure, it seems strange that he should have made himself a party to the disappearance of a portion of it. It may be that the statement he made had not been verified by him, and it may have been altogether erroneous. It is pleasant to find that both Dr Thirlwall and Mr Grote incline to acquit him of this mean dishonesty.

It may be worth while to mention a story told by Plutarch about this painful passage in the life of Demosthenes. Like many of his stories, it is probably a pure fiction, but it is at least amusing. Harpalus, he tells us, won over the orator to his side by sending him a singularly beautiful golden cup, his admiration of which he had noted. Along with the cup were twenty talents, the sum with which the Areopagus had debited him. Shortly afterwards, when the proposals of Harpalus were being discussed in the Assembly, Demosthenes, who had previously opposed them, appeared with a

woollen bandage round his throat, and pretended that
he could not speak, from an attack of quinsy. Some
wag remarked that it must be the silver quinsy. The
people laughed, but were angry. Such is the story.
But, as a fact, Demosthenes did not drop his opposition
to Harpalus. It was on his motion, as we have seen, that
Harpalus was arrested and his treasure sequestrated.

We left the great orator in exile at Trœzen. He was
recalled soon after the death of Alexander in 323 B.C.
An attempt was then made once more to rid Greece of
the Macedonian ascendancy. It was finally crushed
by Antipater in the battle of Crannon in 322 B.C. The
conqueror demanded the surrender of the leading anti-
Macedonian orators—Demosthenes, of course, among
them. Athens from this moment ceased to exist as a
free state. A Macedonian garrison was introduced;
there was a wholesale disfranchisement of citizens,
and a new political constitution was imposed on the
city. Demosthenes did not remain to be a witness of
this degradation. He had been welcomed back to his
native Athens with joyful enthusiasm; now he must
leave her for ever. He took refuge in the little island
of Calauria, off the coast of Argolis. It was here that
he chose to die rather than fall into the hands of the
"exile-hunters," as the emissaries of Antipater were
called. Within the precincts of an ancient temple of
Neptune, regarded of old as an inviolable sanctuary,
he swallowed poison, retaining in his last moments
sufficient presence of mind to expire outside the sacred
enclosure, to which, in Greek belief, death would have
been a pollution.

CHAPTER XIV.

DEMOSTHENES AT THE BAR.

IT has seemed most convenient not to interrupt our sketch of the political career of Demosthenes with any allusions to his purely forensic engagements. He became, comparatively early in life—that is to say, when he was probably under thirty years of age—a very successful pleader in large practice. It may be as well now to give the reader some idea of the work with which he was occupied, and of the speeches which in this capacity he was called on to deliver.

At Athens there was no separate and distinct class answering to our bar. But there were professional orators and rhetoricians in abundance, who made it their business to compose speeches for plaintiffs and defendants. They did not, however, as a rule, make the speeches themselves; they merely prepared them and put them in the hands of their clients, who committed them to memory and then addressed the court. Of course it would often happen that a man felt himself quite unequal to such an ordeal, and would get an experienced speaker to plead for him. Most, however, of the forensic speeches of Demosthenes which have

come down to us, were written for delivery by the
plaintiff or the defendant in person. Part of the
orator's art consisted in adapting them to the style and
manner of man his client happened to be. This cir-
cumstance often gives piquancy to these speeches.
They abound in amusing passages illustrative of
many varieties of Athenian life. We have descrip-
tive touches of the peculiar ways of the commercial
rogue, of the money-lender, of the fraudulent trustee.
Fortune has been kind in preserving for us something
like thirty orations of Demosthenes, in which these and
kindred figures present themselves to our notice. We
thus peep into the banking-house and the factory, and
see the Athenian citizen bargaining with merchants and
shipowners, or busy with his farm, or making his last
will and testament.

Athens was a city in which lawsuits could not fail
to be plentiful. It was a centre of trade, and a resort
of foreigners from all parts. Then, too, there were the
mines of Laurium along the coast; there were quarries
of marble; and the adjacent seas were famous for their
fisheries. Athenian manufactures, too, were highly
prized. From the shores of the Black Sea and the
islands of the Ægean there was a good trade in corn,
timber, wine, and wool. Here were all the materials
of commerce, and consequently of litigation. Many
an Athenian citizen was himself in business; and the
city seems to have swarmed with bustling, enterprising
foreigners who found it convenient to make it their
home. The law courts had plenty of work to do—so
much so, indeed, that the " law's delay " appears to have

been as familiar to Athenians as to ourselves. "Some people," says Xenophen, if he really wrote the treatise attributed to him on the Athenian republic, "complain that a man often waits a twelvemonth at Athens before he can obtain an audience of the Senate or of the popular assembly. The fact is, they have so much to do there that it is impossible to attend to every man's application; some, therefore, are compelled to go away unheard." Ill-natured persons, it seems, hinted that anybody could obtain a hearing by means of a bribe. Xenophon admits that there may be some truth in this; but he adds, speaking from his own knowledge, "that for no amount of gold and silver which could be offered would it be possible for the Athenians to transact all the business that is brought before them." Athens, in fact, was the place to which nearly all causes from the islands of the Ægean were brought for trial; and to which, too, it was probably best and safest that they should be brought. Athenian trials were conducted in a way which to us seems singular, and which at first sight might appear very unfavourable to the administration of justice. Causes were heard, as with us, before juries; but at Athens a jury commonly numbered 500, and might number 1000 or even more. It was, in fact, trial before a popular assembly. There was a president, but he was not armed with the controlling powers of an English judge. Everything was left to the jury; the law of the case as well as the facts was for them to decide. To us this may seem the height of absurdity; but still at Athens it worked moderately well, and in a majority of cases we may believe that it secured at

least substantial justice. The Athenian juror, it is
true, had not received what we call a legal education ;
but he was naturally critical and sharp-witted, and he
was well practised in the hearing of causes.   It is quite
possible that the average decisions of an Athenian jury
may have been as good and satisfactory as those of an
English.   There was, of course, a danger of their being
swayed too much at times by political considerations.
But to this we know that an English jury is also liable.
There was another and a worse danger.   The population of Athens was comparatively small ; and so it
would often happen that plaintiff and defendant, and the
case at issue between them, would be well known to the
jurors.   The Athenian pleader was continually appealing to the personal knowledge of the jury, and would
in this manner supplement deficiencies in the evidence.
" He is a scoundrel ; you all know him to be one,"—
this was the sort of language commonly addressed to a
jury at Athens.   Æschines, in prosecuting one Timar-
chus, dwells on the notoriety of the man's guilt and
wickedness—" Such," he says, " is the testimony of the
whole people of Athens, and it is not right that they
should be convicted of perjury."   This strikes us as
a very loose method of procedure.   Yet we find it
repeatedly in the speeches of Demosthenes.   And it is
what we must expect where the judicial system is made
thoroughly democratic.   We must not be surprised at
the savage invective with which the greatest Athenian
orators thought it seemly to interlard their speeches.
Even with us and all our restrictions, advocates contrive
occasionally to indulge in considerable licence, and did

so formerly to a much greater extent ; and it is, perhaps, a question whether some of the most offensive passages in Demosthenes and Æschines might not be paralleled from English pleadings.

Another evil of the Athenian judicial system was the division of responsibility. One out of 500 or 1000 jurors might very well shelter himself under the excuse, that if he decided wrongly from carelessness or partiality, the result would not be much affected. On the other hand, there were advantages which will occur to the minds of those who are acquainted with the history of free institutions. Corruption and bribery cannot have been particularly easy. Nor, again, could anything like intimidation be well practised. The fact, too, that rich and poor were brought together to discharge an important public function, would have a salutary effect. It would make them feel that they were members of one commonwealth, and inspire them with a respect for its laws. It would call out many of their best sentiments, as well as sharpen their intellects. Their decisions may have sometimes been such as we with our modern ideas cannot approve; but, on the whole, it may be assumed that they commanded the confidence of the people. The Athenian may have had a perverse fondness for listening to the wranglings of rival pleaders; but he did his best generally to hear both sides fairly, and to decide rightly. The jury system, with all its accompaniments of trained oratory and carefully-composed speeches, was contemporaneous with the marvellous development of Athenian literature in the age of Pericles. To it we are certainly indebted for some of the most splendid monuments of human genius.

Such numerous juries could hardly have been fit to deal with cases involving a multitude of intricate details connected with money accounts or valuations of property. Matters of this kind were usually referred, as with us, to a court of arbitration — public arbitrators being annually appointed. Of these we hear continually in the forensic speeches of the Athenian orators, and we may take it for granted that much of the law business was disposed of by them. Indeed, it was the regular practice to submit ordinary private disputes to arbitrators in the first instance; but, as might have been expected in a democratic state, there was always an appeal from their decisions to a jury.

On the whole, it is not unlikely that justice was fairly well administered in the Athenian courts. Such, at all events, seems to have been the opinion of the Greek world; and we can hardly suppose that that opinion was without foundation. Some of the drawbacks of the system have been already noted, and they were no doubt considerable. A clever and unscrupulous advocate might have had a better chance at Athens than he would have with us. It is, of course, an immense advantage that a trained lawyer should preside over a court, and sum up the case, and point out to the jury the general principles by which they should be guided. It is probable that the want of this was often felt at Athens, and led occasionally to unfortunate results. Still, we may be sure that the average Athenian was

a man of intelligence, and perfectly open to reason.
Practice, too, made him tolerably well acquainted with
his country's laws. It is the greatest mistake to conceive of Athens as "a fierce democracy." Her citizens
were for the most part moderately-cultivated persons,
of a tolerant temper, and willing to obey the laws and
the constitution. A successful Athenian advocate must
have come up to a rather high standard; and if
his invective was sometimes coarse and offensively
personal, it must have been set off by a certain
amount of wit, and have been accompanied with acute
reasoning.

Much of the litigation at Athens arose out of bot-
tomry cases—that is, loans of money on the security of
a ship or of its cargo. Business of this kind was trans-
acted on a great scale; and as the risk was considerable, the interest charged was high—as much sometimes as thirty per cent. There seem to have been endless trickeries connected with it. One of Demosthenes'
speeches, for instance, was on behalf of two joint lenders
who had advanced some money on the security of a
wine cargo. Two brothers, merchants of Phaselis in
Pamphylia, were the borrowers. Phaselis, it appears,
had a very bad commercial reputation; and there were
said to be more actions brought against its traders at
Athens than against all the other traders put together.
In this case Demosthenes' client stated that the borrowers of his money had broken their agreement—"that
they had not shipped the stipulated quantity of wine;
that they had raised a further loan on the same security; that they had not purchased a sufficient return

cargo; that, on their return, they had not entered the regular port of Athens, but had put into a little obscure harbour known as 'Smugglers' Creek;' and that, when the repayment of the loan was demanded, they falsely represented that the vessel had been wrecked." Before the matter was settled, one of the borrowers died, and his property went to his brother, Lacritus, who, according to the lenders' statement, had verbally engaged to see that the loan should be repaid. So Lacritus was sued for the amount, although very possibly he was not legally liable, and may merely have been a "referee" for his brother, and have stated, as such, that to the best of his belief they were solvent. He was a man of some note, having been a pupil of Isocrates, and being himself a rather celebrated teacher of rhetoric. He was, in fact, what the Greeks called a "sophist." On this he seems to have presumed; and he went about bragging of his connection with "the great Isocrates." Demosthenes makes his client say: "These sophists are 'a bad lot.' It is no affair of mine if a man chooses to be a sophist, and to pay fees to Isocrates; but they must not, because they think themselves clever, be allowed to swindle other people out of their money. Lacritus does not trust to the justice of his case; but he thinks that, as he has learnt oratory, he shall be able to make you think exactly what he pleases. Perhaps, as he is so clever, he will undertake to prove that black is white—that the money was never borrowed at all—or that it has been paid—or that the bond is waste paper—or that the borrowers had a right to use our money as they liked." It is possible, as has

been supposed, that Demosthenes is really hitting at
Isocrates in his abuse of Lacritus.

In one of his speeches he argues against the right of
a man to take a name already borne by one of his
brothers. The case is a rather singular one. Mantitheus, the son of Mantias, brings an action against his
half-brother Bœotus for having got himself registered
as Mantitheus. Bœotus was the son of Mantias by a
mistress, herself an Athenian citizen, and so capable,
according to Athenian law, of transmitting citizenship
to her offspring. Every citizen's child was enrolled or
registered on the citizen-list at an early age, and then
again subsequently on reaching manhood. Bœotus
received his name on the first of these occasions. Before the second registration had taken place, his father
died. Disliking the name, which suggested a familiar
Greek proverb, "like a Bœotian hog," he contrived on
this second occasion to get himself enrolled under his
brother's name of Mantitheus. In this manner the
legal designation of the two brothers became the same.
It should be noted that at Athens a citizen was described by his own name, by that of his father, and
that of his parish or township—Attica being divided
into so many townships, or *demes*, as they were called.
In a comparatively small community this might not
be inconvenient. What, however, Bœotus had done,
could hardly fail to lead to confusion. His half-
brother, in the speech composed for him by Demosthenes, hints that matters would be all the worse, as
Bœotus kept rather questionable company. Unpleasant
mistakes, too, as he points out, would probably arise

out of unpaid debts and appearances in the law courts.
In fact, the son of the lawful wife would often be
credited with the scrapes into which the son of the
mistress was likely to get himself.

"You tiresome Bœotus," says Demosthenes' client,
who really seems to have been a much-injured man,
"I would wish you, if possible, to renounce all
your bad ways ; but if that is too much to hope,
pray oblige me to this extent : cease to give yourself trouble ; cease to harass me with litigation ; be
content that you have gained a franchise, a property,
a father. No one seeks to dispossess you ; nor do
I.   If, as you pretend to be a brother, you act
like a brother, people will believe that you are my
kinsman.   But if you plot against me, go to law with
me, envy me, slander me, it will be thought that you
have intruded into a strange family, and treat the
members as if they were alien to you. As to me personally, however wrong my father may have been in
refusing to acknowledge you, I certainly am innocent.
It was not my business to know who were his sons ;
it was for him to show me whom I was to regard as
brothers. As long as he forebore to acknowledge you,
I held you no kinsman ; ever since he acknowledged
you, I have regarded you as he did. You have had
your portion of the inheritance after my father's death ;
you participate in our religious worship, in our civil
rights—no one excludes you from these.   What woul l
you have ? Whoever hears the name will have to ask
which of us two are meant ; then, if the person means

you, he will reply, 'The one whom Mantias was compelled to adopt.' Do you wish for this?"

We pass to quite a different case. It is a dispute between two neighbouring Attic farmers.* Their
holdings were in a hilly part of Attica, and were
separated by a public road. It is an action for damages
which the plaintiff, Callicles, alleged that he had sustained through the obstruction of a water-course, which
carried off the drainage from the surrounding hills.
The defendant's father had built a wall on his land,
with the view of diverting the water into the road.
It seems that in Attica a proprietor might turn off his
drainage into a public way, to the great detriment, as
may well be supposed, of the country roads, which, in
hilly districts, must at times have been almost impas-
sable. The effect of the wall in this case was, that
after heavy rains the plaintiff's farm was overflowed,
as well as the road. For this the plaintiff brought his
action. The defendant, Demosthenes' client, pleaded
in justification that the wall in question had been law-
fully erected by his father fifteen years ago; that no
objection was then raised by the plaintiff's family;
that the so-called water-course was not really a water-
course, but was part of his own land, as it was planted
with fruit-trees, and contained an old family burial-
ground. The stream, too, which caused the mischief,
did not come to the defendant from a neighbour's
farm; it flowed down the road both above and below
him: the flood which it occasioned in wet weather was

* Speech against Callicles.

a natural misfortune, from which others had suffered as
well as the plaintiff—only, they had never thought of
going to law about it. The defendant broadly hints
that the plaintiff has an eye to his property, and is
trying to oust him from it by a vexatious action. The
matter in dispute was trifling enough, and the jury
must have been inclined to laugh at the solemnity with
which they were implored to give their best attention
to all the details of the case. " There is no greater
nuisance" (so the defendant begins his pleading) " than
a covetous neighbour, which it has been my lot to
meet with. Callicles has set his heart on my land, and
worries me with litigation. First he got his cousin to
claim it from me, but I defeated that claim. I beseech
you all to hear me with attention—not because I am
any speaker, but that you may learn by the facts how
groundless the action is." After he has explained the
facts, he asks pathetically what he is to do with the
water, if he may not drain it off either into the public
road or into private ground. " Surely," he adds, with
a touch of bucolic humour, " the plaintiff won't force
me to drink it up?" The damage done could not have
been very ruinous, if we may judge from a single
specimen. It appears that the mothers of the two
litigants used to visit each other, as country neighbours;
and on one occasion, when the defendant's mother was
calling at the plaintiff's house, she found the family
plunged in the deepest distress, and apparently crushed
by some more than ordinary calamity. It would seem
that the rustic mind then, as now, was peculiarly
sensitive to the most ludicrously trifling loss, and

delighted in describing it with the most violent exag-
geration. The injured farmer's wife, on this occasion,
pointed with tears to four bushels of barley which had
got wet and were being dried, and to a jar of oil,
which had indeed fallen down, but which was not
damaged. For this they wanted to claim, according to
the defendant, 1000 drachms, or about £40, by way of
compensation. An Attic farmer, it would seem (like
his English representative), was not likely to suffer
from asking too little. There is something very
characteristic in the following remark, which Demosthenes' client makes about his opponent: "In going
to law with me," he says, " I hold the plaintiff to be
thoroughly wicked and infatuated."

In another * somewhat interesting case, Demosthenes
pleads for an unfortunate man who had been ejected
from his township, and was thereby in danger of ceasing
to be an Athenian citizen. At Athens, citizenship was
the subject of the strictest scrutiny; and the registers of
the townships were kept with the utmost care. Every
citizen, as has been already noted, had to be twice
registered ; and to insure accuracy, and to exclude
questionable persons, the lists were from time to time
revised. Even with all these precautions, cases of
disputed citizenship not unfrequently occurred. In
the case which we are about to consider, Demosthenes'
client had been struck off the register of his township
on the occasion of a revision. The man's father had
been taken prisoner during the latter part of the Peloponnesian War; and having lived some years "in for-

* Speech against Eubulides.

eign parts," he spoke Attic rather indifferently. However, on his return to Athens, he had resumed his
citizenship; and transmitted it, without question, as
it is alleged, to his son. He was very poor, and he
and his wife had to eke out a livelihood by the
humblest of occupations. His son, it seems, had
made enemies in his parish, and among them one
Eubulides, against whom he had given evidence in a
court of justice. Eubulides, when he became mayor
of the township, had the registers revised, and contrived to get the man's name struck off. He managed
this by a sort of trick. The revision of the register
took place at Athens, from which the township was
about five miles distant. A good deal of time was
wasted in making speeches and drawing up resolutions; and the case of Demosthenes' client was taken
last of all. It was now dark, and all but about thirty
members of the township had gone home—and these,
it is said, were in the interest of Eubulides. When
the poor man's name was called, Eubulides started to
his feet, assailed him with a volley of abuse, and
insisted on a vote of expulsion. It was useless to ask
for an adjournment; the business was hurried through,
and sixty ballot-balls were found in the box against
him, though it seems that only thirty townsmen were
present. The result was utter ruin to the man. Loss
of citizenship meant social death, and probably slavery.
He makes through his counsel a piteous appeal to the
jury, and says that if their verdict is adverse he shall
commit suicide, that he may at least have the satisfaction of being buried by his relatives in his native

country. " I have been shamefully treated by this
Eubulides "—so he begins ; " and I pray you, considering the great importance of the present trial, and the
disgrace and ruin which attend conviction, to hear me,
as you have my opponent, in silence." Further on in
his speech he touches on his poverty, and the humble
way in which his family maintain themselves.

" We confess that we sell ribbons, and live not in the
way we could wish. We are so low down in the world
that our opponent may go out of his way to abuse us.
It seems to me that our trafficking in the market-place
is the strongest proof of the falsity of this man's
charges. My mother, he says, sold ribbons in the
market-place. Well, if she was an alien, they should
have inspected the market tolls, and shown whether
she paid the alien's toll, and to what country she
belonged. If she was a slave, the person who bought
her, or the person who sold her, should have been
called to give evidence. Then he has said she was a
nurse. We do not deny she was, in those evil days*
when all our people were badly off. But you will find
many women who are citizens taking children to nurse.
Of course, if we had been rich, we should not have
sold ribbons, or have been at all in distress. But
what has that to do with my descent ? Pray do not
scorn the poor (their poverty is a sufficient misfortune
for them), much less those who try to get an honest
livelihood. Poverty compels free men to do many
mean and servile acts, for which they deserve to be

* The last years of the Peloponnesian War.

pitied rather than to be ruined. They tell me that many women, citizens by birth, have become both nurses and wool-dressers and vintagers, owing to the misfortunes of our country at that period. I have confidence in my case, and I come as an appellant to your tribunal for protection. I know that the courts of law are more powerful not only than my fellow-townsmen, but even than the Council of the popular Assembly; and justly so—for your verdicts are in every respect most righteous."

He concludes his address to the jury with the threat of suicide already mentioned

One more of these cases must suffice. It is an amusing one—an action, as we should say, for assault and battery. There were, it seems, occasional outbursts of rowdyism even at refined Athens, and the police were not always "on the spot" to repress them. Some of the "fast" young men about town formed themselves into clubs—like the "Mohock Club" of the last century, whose lawless proceedings are the subject of one of the numbers of the 'Spectator.'* "An outrageous ambition (as the 'Spectator' says) of doing all possible hurt to their fellow-creatures was the great cement of their assemblies, and the only qualification required in the members." There was a club at Athens which called itself the Triballi, the name of one of the wildest and most savage tribes of Thrace. The members of this delightful fraternity used to commit all manner of horrid and indecent outrages on inoffensive

* No. 324.

citizens as they were taking the evening air or returning home from parties. One Conon and his sons
specially distinguished themselves. Their victim on
one occasion retained Demosthenes for his counsel.
They had all been on foreign military service together,
and it was then that the practical jokes and annoy-
ances were begun of which Demosthenes' client complains. Conon and his set would drink all day after
lunch; and so by dinner-time they were only fit for
drunken frolics. " At first," the plaintiff says, " they
played tricks on his servants; at last on himself and
his party. They would pretend that our servants
annoyed them with smoke in cooking, and were saucy;
then they beat them, and played all sorts of dirty,
brutal jokes on them. We expressed our disgust;
and when they insulted us, we all went in a body to
the general, who gave them a severe reprimand." In
this manner a very sore feeling grew up; and when
they all returned to Athens, the assault took place
which was the ground of the action.

" When I had got back to Athens," the plaintiff
says, " I was taking a walk one evening in the
market - place with a friend of my own age, when
Ctesias, Conon's son, passed us, very much intoxicated. Seeing us, he made an exclamation like
a drunken man muttering something indistinctly
to himself, and went on his way. There was a
drinking - party near, at the house of Pamphilus,
the fuller. Conon and many others were there.
Ctesias got them to leave the party and go with him

to the market-place. We were near the Leccorium"
(a small temple) "when we encountered them. As we
came up, one of them rushed on my friend and held
him. Conon and another tripped up my heels, and
threw me into the mud, and jumped on me, and
kicked me with such violence that my lip was cut
through and my eye closed up. In this plight they
left me, unable to rise or speak. As I lay I heard
them use dreadful language, some of which I should
be sorry to repeat to you. One thing you shall hear.
It proves Conon's malice, and that he was the ring-
leader in the affair. He crowed, mimicking fighting-
cocks when they have won a battle; and his companions
bade him clap his elbows against his sides, like wings.
I was afterwards found by some persons who came
that way, and carried home without my cloak, which
these men had carried off. When they got to the
door, my mother and the maid-servants began crying
and bewailing. I was carried with some difficulty to
a bath ; they washed me all over, and then showed me
to the doctor."

It seems to have struck Demosthenes that possibly
some of the jury would be inclined to laugh at this
somewhat ludicrously pathetic picture.

"Will you laugh," he makes his client say, "and
let Conon off, because he says we are a band of merry
fellows who, in our adventures and amours, strike and
break the neck of any one we please? I trust
not. None of you would have laughed if you had
been present when I was dragged and stripped and
kicked, and carried to the home which I had left

strong and well; and my mother rushed out, and the women cried and wailed as if a man had died in the house, so that some of the neighbours sent to ask what was the matter."

Conon and his associates may well have been a terror to peaceable citizens, if we may trust the following little sketch of their proceedings:—

"Many of you know the set. There's the grey-headed man, who all day long has a solemn frown on his brows, and wears a coarse mantle and single-soled shoes. But when they get together, they stick at no wickedness or disgraceful conduct. These are their fine and spirited sayings: 'Shan't we bear witness for one another?' 'Doesn't it become friends and comrades?' 'What will he bring against you that you're afraid of?' 'Some men say they saw him beaten?' We'll say, 'You never touched him.' 'Stripped of his coat?' We'll say, 'They began.' 'His lip was sewed up?' We'll say, 'Your head was broken.' Remember," solemnly adds the plaintiff, "I produce medical evidence; they do not—for they can get no evidence against me but what is furnished by themselves."

It is to be hoped that the jury did not laugh, but were persuaded by Demosthenes to make an example of such offenders. Blackguardism could hardly go further than to rob a man of his cloak, in addition to beating and kicking him. The Athenian rowdy, if Conon and his set were fair and average types of the genus, certainly deserved little mercy.

CONCLUSION.

DEMOSTHENES is one of those men concerning whom, both as a statesman and an orator, there cannot be much difference of opinion. As a statesman, he is unanimously eulogised by modern historians of the first rank—such as Thirlwall, Grote, and Curtius. Every one who sees anything to esteem and admire in old Greek life, must esteem and admire Demosthenes. His political career was a consistent one. He clung to and worked for one idea. That idea was a free and independent Greece, of which his own Athens had, morally and intellectually, the right to be head. It was not, as we have seen, the view of Isocrates; nor was it afterwards that of the historian Polybius. Both these men refused to believe that Greece could any longer be what she had been. Both were honest and conscientious thinkers; but we can never have quite the same feeling towards the man who is inclined to despair of a great cause as we have towards him who will persist in hoping against hope. It was this which Demosthenes did through life amid many discouragements; and this gives him a moral greatness which we believe posterity will always recognise. Such a man